Advanced Apex Programming for Salesforce.com and Force.com

Second Edition

By

Dan Appleman

Desaware Publishing
San Jose, California

Editor: Marian Kicklighter

Second Edition

ISBN: 978-1-936754-07-6
Library of Congress Control Number: 2013951620

Printed in the United States of America*.

www.AdvancedApex.com

* Copies purchased in countries outside of the U.S. may have been printed locally using print on demand technology.

Contents

Introduction

This book is not a rehash of the Salesforce Apex language documentation.

I just wanted to get that out of the way. I know there is sometimes value in the kind of book where 90% of the content is a rephrasing of the documentation and only 10% is new and interesting – a good author can organize information to make it easier for beginners to learn. But they are frustrating for intermediate and advanced developers who have to sift endlessly through familiar content to find one or two nuggets of new material.

So I'm going to assume that you either have read, or can read, the Force.com Apex language documentation. If you are new to Apex, you will find this book helpful – especially if you are coming to Apex from another language, but it is not a tutorial and will not replace the Apex documentation. If you have Apex programming experience, I'm confident you'll find material here that will at the very least prove thought provoking, if not occasionally mind-blowing.

This book is about design patterns, best practices, and creative solutions to the kinds of problems developers face out in the real world.

You see, language documentation is generally written by the language team (or their technical writers) – which is good, because they know the language best. But the language team members are rarely application developers – that's not their job.

White-papers and application notes are generally written by technical evangelists and consultants who often do have real-world experience, but are limited by the focus and format of the particular white paper or article. Short articles (of which I've written many) serve a purpose, but are often limited in the level of depth they can achieve.

If you want to bring together real-world experience in a format that allows for as much depth as necessary, and organizes the information in such a way that concepts build on each other to really teach the material – you need a book. You need a book written by someone who actually writes production code, both as a consultant for individual clients, and as a developer of applications for distribution.

Which brings me to the story how I came to write this book.

For most of my career, I was a software developer on Microsoft platforms – first C, then C++, then Visual Basic, then VB .NET and C#. I ran (and still run) the company Desaware, that creates add-on products for Visual Studio developers (desaware.com). I also wrote a number of programming books, and spent quite a few years on the speaker circuit - presenting topics at conferences that focused on Microsoft technologies.

About six years ago, a Salesforce consultant I know needed an Apex trigger written, and since I was one of the few programmers she knew, she asked me to take a look. Writing that first trigger was certainly easy enough – though I suspect I'd be embarrassed by the code if I looked at it now. I found myself spending more and more time working in Apex – I found it to be both challenging and fun.

About three years ago, I joined her and two others to establish a new company, Full Circle CRM, to develop a new Salesforce application related to marketing and sales data and analytics. Visit fullcirclecrm.com if you're curious about the details. As CTO, I designed and built the application – which evolved into a very large and sophisticated native AppExchange app (an app that runs entirely on the force.com platform). In doing so, I learned a lot.

As I have always enjoyed sharing what I learn, I ended up writing this book. It contains all of the things that I wish I had known six years ago when I first started working in Apex. Things that I learned the hard way. Things that are either not found in the documentation, or are hidden in a footnote somewhere when they should be plastered across an entire page in bold flashing neon.

Think of this as a companion to the Apex Language reference – a commentary if you will. The focus is on the core language and design patterns. These are the essential foundations that you need to work effectively in Apex with the various platform features such as VisualForce, Chatter, and so forth (topics that are important, and deserving of their own books, but are not covered here).

Parts of this book focus on concepts – ways of thinking that will be fairly easy to follow, even for relative beginners and those completely new to Apex. But parts of this book focus more on advanced design patterns, and to really understand them, you'll need to dig into the code, and preferably install and experiment with the samples. You may even need to refer back to the language documentation. You may even find parts of the book to be too hard to follow on a first reading. In truth, the book would hardly deserve the word "Advanced" in the title if this were not the case. If you do find yourself getting stuck, skip or scan a section and then move on. You'll find it easier to digest the second time through.

By the time you're done, I think you will find it was well worth the effort.

Dan Appleman

dan@desawarepublishing.com

Sample Code

You can download the sample code for this book from the book's website at AdvancedApex.com/samplecode. It is provided as an unmanaged package.

An unmanaged package is a great way to distribute code, but poses certain problems with regards to sample code, in that many of the examples demonstrate errors that would prevent installation of the software, and many of them duplicate functionality and aren't designed to work together.

As a result, much of the code in the samples has been commented out – you will need to uncomment the appropriate parts of the code, and comment out parts you are not using, in order to use the sample code. This makes it possible to distribute all of the samples in one unmanaged package and still pass the required unit tests.

You will need to install the sample code to follow some of the content in this book – the book does not contain the complete listings of all of the sample code.

The following is a quick reference of which classes, triggers and test classes are used by the various chapters in the book.

Chapter 2:
- Classes – SomeFutureOperations, ThinkingInApex
- Trigger – OnOpportunity1
- Test Classes – TestThinkingInApex

Chapter 3:
- Classes – Benchmarking
- Test Classes – TestThinkingInApexLimits

Chapter 4:

- Classes – ThinkingInApexBulkPatterns, BulkPatternBatch
- Trigger – OnOpportunity2
- Test Classes - TestBulkPatterns

Chapter 5
- Test Classes – FunWithCollections

Chapter 6

- Classes – TriggerArchitectureClass1, TriggerArchitectureClass2, TriggerArchitectureMain, TriggerExamples
- Trigger – OnOpportunity2
- Test Classes – TestTriggersExample

Chapter 7
- Classes – GoingAsync, GoingAsync2, ScheduledDispatcher
- Trigger – SolutionTrigger1, OnLeadForGoingAsync2
- Test Classes – TestGoingAsync, TestGoingAsync2

Chapter 8

- Classes – GoingAsync2, Concurrency1, ScheduledDispatcher

- Test Classes – TestGoingAsync2

Chapter 9, 10
- Classes – DiagnosticsMain, DiagnosticsTriggers1, DiagnosticsTriggers2, DiagnosticsInstrumentation, AppConfigSupport
- Trigger – OnOpportunity3

- Test Classes – TestDiagnostics1, TestDiagnostics2

Chapter 11

- Classes – PersonAccountSupport
- Triggers – OnContact1, OnAccount1
- Test Classes – TestForManaged, TestPersonAccount

Advanced Apex Programming for Salesforce.com and Force.com

Second Edition

Part I – Thinking in Apex

What is a computer language?

Ok, I know - that's a stupid question to start with. Of course you know what a computer language is. If you didn't, you'd hardly be reading a book that claims to be an advanced programming book.

At the same time, it's a useful question for exactly that reason. Because you do know what a computer language is, you'll probably be grateful if I don't waste your time answering that question. In fact, it brings to mind a long list of questions and introductory material that are not worth discussing at all, either because you should know them, or because you can easily find them in the documentation.

So let's begin with a partial list of material that I won't try to teach you.

Beyond Syntax

When we talk about computer languages in the context of actual software development, we're really talking about three different things:

- Language syntax – the actual text of the language.
- Language semantics – what that text does when it executes.
- Language platform (or framework) – what resources are available to the language, and how does the language interact with the underlying system.

Of these, this book will almost completely ignore the first item. If you've used Apex at all, you're probably well familiar with its syntax. If you are migrating from another language, suffice to say that Apex is syntactically similar to Java or C#, with most of the constructs you would expect from a modern object oriented language, including support for single inheritance, interfaces, and some template support that you will probably never actually use.

In terms of semantics, we'll largely ignore the core language semantics. Most of the language constructs: control flow structures, operators, variable declarations, and so on, work exactly as you would expect.

In fact, Apex is so similar to other languages, that at first glance you might think that it will be a quick and easy migration. And in truth, it can be an easy migration – but only if you recognize a few areas that are not only different, but different in huge, fundamental ways.

Most of this book will be dealing with the third item on the list – the interaction of the language with the platform. But the rest of this part of the book will focus on the four key concepts that you must understand in order to succeed in Apex programming:

- Execution Contexts
- Static Variables
- Bulk Patterns
- Limits

These concepts dominate every aspect of software development under Apex. Because of these concepts, Apex programming involves radically different design patterns and architectures than Java and C#, even though their syntax and even semantics are similar.

In a way, this is like learning a spoken language. You can memorize words and phrases. But you don't really know the language until you start thinking and dreaming in it. My goal in this chapter is to help you take the words and phrases that you know from the reference documentation or other languages, and learn to think in Apex.

1 – The Execution Context

The execution context is one of the key defining concepts in Apex programming. It influences every aspect of software development on the Force.com platform.

An execution context has two characteristics:

- It defines the scope and lifetime of static variables.
- It defines the context for those governor limits that are re-set between execution contexts.

I'll be discussing both static variables and limits in more depth later. For now, the key facts to remember (and I assure you, once you start working in Apex, you will never forget them) are:

- Static variables are maintained throughout an execution context, and are unique to an execution context.
- Many (but not all) limits are reset between execution contexts. For example, if governor limits restrict you to 100 database queries in an execution context, each execution context can have 100 database queries. Different types of execution contexts may have different limits.
- You can know when an execution context starts. You generally can't know when it ends.

Running Apex Code

An execution context begins when one of a number of possible external events or operations happen that have the ability to start running Apex code. These include:

- A database trigger: Triggers can occur on insertion, update, deletion or undeletion of many standard Salesforce objects and all custom objects.

- Future call (asynchronous call): Future calls can be requested from Apex code. They run with extended limits.

- Scheduled Apex: You can implement an Apex class that can be called by the system on a scheduled basis.

- Batch Apex: You can implement a class designed to process large numbers of database records.

- Web service: You can implement a class that can be accessed via SOAP or REST from an external site or from JavaScript on a web page.

- VisualForce: Your VisualForce pages can execute Apex code in VisualForce controllers to retrieve or set page properties or execute methods.

- Global Apex: You can expose a global method that can be called from other Apex code.

- Anonymous Apex: Apex code can be compiled and executed dynamically from the Developer Console, Force.com IDE or through an external web-service call.

When Apex code starts executing as a result of any of these events or operations, it runs within an execution context. If the event or operation was caused by Apex code, or is part of a system process, the code will continue to run in the same execution context that caused the event or operation.

I know that sounds confusing. Let's look at some examples.

Consider the simple case of a trigger on the update of a Lead object. In the trivial case of an absolutely new organization with just one trigger, the execution context begins when your trigger code begins to run, and ends when your code exits as shown in Figure 1-1.

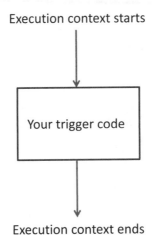

Figure 1-1 – Simple execution context

What if you have multiple triggers on lead insertion? This is not uncommon. Code in organizations tends to evolve over time, and it's very common for one developer to build a new trigger on the same event, rather than risk modifying (and breaking) trigger code written by another developer. Now you can end up with the scenario shown in Figure 1-2.

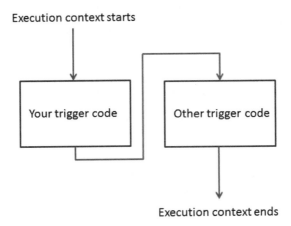

Figure 1-2 –Execution context with two triggers

As you can see, both triggers run in the same execution context. So they share the same set of limits (as long as they are in the same application – more on that later), and the same set of static variables.

This seems simple enough. But what if this particular organization has a workflow on the lead that does a field update? Now you may end up with the scenario shown in Figure 1-3.

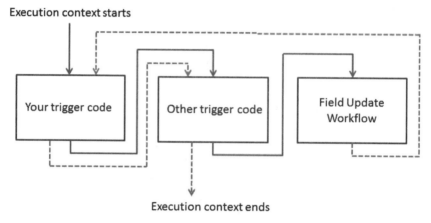

Figure 1-3 –Execution context with two triggers and a workflow

As you can see, the field update workflow not only runs in the same execution context, it can cause the triggers to execute again within the same context.

This brings up an interesting question. How can you know if your trigger is executing for the first time, or if it is executing again for the same update because of a workflow or other trigger?

This is where static variables come into play. Remember, their lifetime and scope is defined by the execution context. So if you had a static variable defined in a class "myclass" thus:

```
public Static Boolean firstcall = false;
```

You could use the following design pattern in your trigger to determine if this was the first or subsequent call for this execution context.

```
if(!myclass.firstcall)
{
    // First call into trigger
    myclass.firstcall = true;
}
else
{
    // Subsequent call into trigger
}
```

This design pattern turns out to be extremely important, as you will see later.

Let's consider the ramifications of what you have just seen:

- You can have multiple triggers on an event, but have no control over the order in which they execute.
- Limits are shared within an Execution Context, thus you may be sharing limits with other code over which you have no control and which may be added after yours is built and tested.
- Workflows, which can be created by non-programmers, can impact the order and execution of your Apex code in unpredictable ways, even causing your code to execute again for the same object and within the same execution context.

At this point, if you are coming to Apex from another language, you might be feeling a certain amount of shock. On other platforms, you, the developer, are largely in control of your application. User input may be unpredictable and have to be accounted for, but you know how to do that. It's not as if users can modify the underlying behavior of the application, or add code that interacts with your application. Even if you do have a plug-in model or API, those using it will be (hopefully) knowledgeable and expected to follow your specifications, guidelines and documentation.

But Salesforce.com was designed to minimize the need for custom software. The Salesforce.com logo is "no software". So there are a great many things that users can do that can impact the code that you write. Because execution contexts are shared, there are things that other developers can do that can impact the code that you write.

And by impact, I mean break.

But don't let this thought scare you. You'll quickly adjust to the idea that your finely crafted code can be broken by a junior system administrator writing a careless validation rule. It's just part of the territory – and part of what makes Apex coding a fun challenge.

My point here isn't to scare you, but to emphasize my earlier point. Apex may look like Java, but because of fundamental platform differences, it requires a different set of design patterns and different approaches for architecting applications.

2 – Static Variables

In most computer languages, a class static variable is essentially a global variable that is associated with a particular class. That means that it exists regardless of whether you've actually created an instance of the class, and that a single instance of the variable is shared by all instances of the class and, in fact, by the entire application.

So, for example, if you had the following class:

```
public class myclass {
    public static int myclassstatic;
}
```

You could access `myclass.myclassstatic` anywhere in your code and always access the same variable. Developers are accustomed to using static variables in a variety of design patterns, such as sharing data between classes, counting or maintaining lists of class instances (objects), or as a way of organizing and controlling access to general purpose global variables. Developers of multithreaded applications also know to take care to synchronize access to static variables, in order to avoid race conditions or data corruption.

That's the case with Java, C#, C++, VB .NET and virtually every block structured language.

Except for Apex.

The difference between static variables in Apex and most other languages is simple in concept, but has a huge impact on the way they are used.

Static variables in Apex have execution context scope and lifetime.

In other words, static variables can only be accessed from within the execution context in which they are created, and are deleted when the execution context completes.

Let's first consider what this means in terms of traditional static variable design patterns.

- Static variables do not persist information between execution contexts. They cannot be used to keep track of the overall execution of your application, or to cache data or objects for use while your application is running. In fact, Apex does not support the equivalent of application or session variables at all. Anything you wish to persist must be stored in database objects or custom settings (more on that later).
- There is no need for synchronization. A given execution context runs on a single thread, so static variables are, in effect, the equivalent of thread local storage – each thread has its own copy of these variables and there is no need to synchronize access. Which is a good thing; given that Apex has no real synchronization objects.

But if Apex eliminates some design patterns that are common in other languages, it offers some new ones that are essential for every Apex developer to understand.

Maintaining Data Across Trigger Invocations

Earlier in this chapter, you saw an example of how a static variable could be used to remember that you had already executed the code in an after-update trigger.

Here's another common design pattern.

Let's say you have a computationally intensive operation that you wish to perform in a number of different scenarios. For example, reassigning account ownership based on some rules a user has defined. You might want to do this after a field value has changed on the account, or any of its contacts or opportunities.

It's very common to move longer operations into future calls – asynchronous operations that can be queued by your code. Future calls execute at some indeterminate time in the future, but because the platform can schedule them based on server load, they are granted higher limits than other execution contexts, and are thus ideal for computationally intensive tasks.

You can only make up to ten future calls from an execution context, and you can't make a future call from a future context. Because your code may share an execution context with other code, ideally you only want to invoke your future call once.

So in this scenario, you wish to initiate your future call from a number of different triggers or conditions. How can you keep track of whether or not you have already initiated the call? The answer: use a static variable.

But how do you use it? You can't use it as a flag to indicate that a future call is required. That's because in Apex you have no way of knowing that you are exiting an execution context. You can, however, use it as a flag to indicate that the call has already been made.

Here's a typical implementation of this design pattern:

```
public class SomeFutureOperations {

    private static Boolean FutureCallCalled = false;

    public static void DoFutureCall()
    {
```

```
    if(FutureCallCalled ||
        System.isFuture()) return;
    FutureCallCalled = true;
    ActualFutureCall();
}


@future
private static void ActualFutureCall()
{
    // Actual async code here
    system.debug('ActualFutureCall async
                operation');
}


}
```

You'll learn more about asynchronous design patterns in Chapter 7.

Caching Data

In the previous example, you saw how a static variable can "remember" a value throughout the duration of an execution context in order to avoid one kind of limit. In this example, you'll see how they can be used to avoid another kind of limit.

Consider the case where you have one or more triggers or methods, and the execution depends in some way on the user who triggered the execution. You might be storing different field values based on the user. Or you might be prohibiting certain operations, or performing additional operations based on the user.

In this scenario, let's say you've added a custom field to the User object, call it UserIsSpecial__c, that controls these operations.

You can retrieve the current value of this field using the following code:

```
User u = [Select UserIsSpecial__c from
          User where ID = :UserInfo.getUserId()];
Boolean UserIsSpecial = u.UserIsSpecial__c;
```

If you were only using this value in one place in your code, this would be fine – you could just use the query as is. But if you intend to use this value across multiple methods and triggers, this approach could result in numerous SOQL operations (SOQL being the database query language for the Force.com platform). The number of allowed SOQL calls is limited within an Execution context – so you want to minimize those calls where possible.

The solution is to cache the value the first time it is used. Rather than try to anticipate where the first use will be (which can be tricky in a complex application), it's best to centralize access of the variable by placing it in an Apex class as follows:

```
public class ThinkingInApex {

    private static Boolean IsUserSpecialChecked =
                      false;
    private static Boolean UserIsSpecial = false;

    public static Boolean IsUserSpecial()
    {
        if(IsUserSpecialChecked) return UserIsSpecial;

        User u = [Select UserIsSpecial__c from User
                where ID = :UserInfo.getUserId()];
        UserIsSpecial = u.UserIsSpecial__c;
        IsUserSpecialChecked = true;
        return UserIsSpecial;
```

```
    }
}
```

Now, you can obtain the user information by calling Think-ingInApex.UserIsSpecial() from anywhere in your code without worrying about making redundant SOQL calls.

It turns out that taking this approach has additional benefits. What if you later decide that you need other information from the user record? Say, the current user's time zone?

You could extend the previous example as follows:

```
public class ThinkingInApex {

    private static Boolean UserCacheLoaded = false;
    private static Boolean UserIsSpecial = false;
    private static String UserTimeZone = null;

    public static Boolean IsUserSpecial()
    {
        if(UserCacheLoaded) return UserIsSpecial;
        CacheUserInfo();
        return UserIsSpecial;
    }

    public static String UserTimeZone()
    {
        if(UserCacheLoaded) return UserTimeZone;
        CacheUserInfo();
        return UserTimeZone;
    }
```

```
private static void CacheUserInfo()
{
    if(UserCacheLoaded) return;
    User u = [Select UserIsSpecial__c,
        TimeZoneSidKey from User where
        ID = :UserInfo.getUserId()];
    UserIsSpecial = u.UserIsSpecial__c;
    UserTimeZone = u.TimeZoneSidKey;
    UserCacheLoaded = true;
}
}
```

With this approach, you can cache all necessary information from an object with only one SOQL call – which is very efficient. Even though the code changes needed to support more than one user field was fairly substantial, it would not have impacted existing code outside of this class. That code continues to call the IsUserSpecial() function.

Generally speaking, using static class methods to centralize access to information that is (or could be) used in more than one place is a good idea. Though it has some small cost in terms of lines of code, the long term benefits of being able to make changes to the sourcing of that information, without requiring widespread changes throughout your code, are enormous.

For example: let's say that a few months after your code was deployed, you suddenly decided that it wasn't the time zone of the current user you cared about, but actually the time zone of the user's supervisor. Or if you wanted to use a specific time zone for users from certain countries. These changes could be made simply by modifying the UserTimeZone() function – you wouldn't have to make any other changes in your application.

There is, however, one caveat to this approach. You can run into trouble if you try to cache large amounts of data. You see, there is also a limit to the size of memory heap you can use in an execution context! If you need to work with larger amounts of data, you may need to requery each time you need the data instead of caching it. And if you are facing both limits – not enough heap space and not enough available SOQL operations, you may need to defer the operation into a future call where you have higher limits.

You'll read more about those kinds of tradeoffs in chapter 3, but first, there is one more static variable design pattern to consider.

Controlling Program Flow

Consider the scenario where you want to enforce that every opportunity is created with an OpportunityContactRole (i.e. has a contact associated with it).

The right way to do this would be to use a VisualForce page to override the New Opportunity button and provide users with a nice warning and explanation that opportunities should only be created from the contact page or through conversion. But you might want to add an extra layer of enforcement by using a trigger that tests for the presence of an OpportunityContactRole on each newly created opportunity, and reports an error if one is missing. One reason for this extra enforcement is that it extends the requirement beyond the user interface to include opportunities created via the API or in other Apex code.

The enforcement code might look something like this:

```
trigger OnOpportunity1 on Opportunity (after insert) {
    ThinkingInApex.AfterInsertOpportunity(
    trigger.new, trigger.newmap);
}
```

```
public class ThinkingInApex {
    public static void AfterInsertOpportunity(
        List<Opportunity> newlist,
        Map<ID, Opportunity> newmap)
    {

        List<OpportunityContactRole> ocrs =
        [SELECT ID, ContactID, IsPrimary,
        OpportunityID from OpportunityContactRole
        where OpportunityID in :newmap.keyset()];

        Set<ID> OcrOpportunities = new Set<ID>();

        for(OpportunityContactRole ocr: ocrs)
            OcrOpportunities.add(ocr.OpportunityID);

        for(Opportunity op: newlist)
        {
            if(! OcrOpportunities.contains(op.id))
            op.addError('Opportunity Contact Role is
            required to create an opportunity');
        }

        // Other functionality
    }
}
```

You may wonder why the validation code is in a separate class instead of in the trigger itself. This will become clear shortly.

This code does work. If you create an opportunity from a contact page, you get the opportunity. If you create the opportunity from anywhere else, you get an error message such as shown in Figure 2-1.

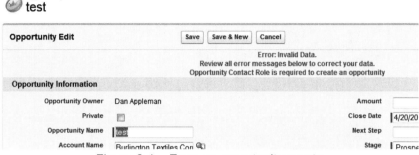

Figure 2-1 – Error on opportunity create

So far, so good. But what about test code? In order to deploy any Apex code into production, you must have unit tests that cover at least 75% of your code. When you create an Opportunity from a contact page, Salesforce magically creates the OpportunityContactRole objects *before* the after-insert trigger. But how can you do that in your test code? The following test code fails:

```
static testMethod void test3()
{
    Opportunity op = new Opportunity( name='optest',
        StageName ='Prospecting',
        CloseDate = Date.Today() );
    insert op;
}
```

This code will test the validation part of this particular trigger. But you need a way to bypass validation in test code in order to test the rest of the trigger code (and for any other unit test that creates an opportunity).

Here is where static variables come into play again. Use a static variable to hold a list of contacts to use for creating OpportunityContactRole objects during tests. Change the class code to the following:

```
public static List<Contact> AssociateContacts = null;

public static void AfterInsertOpportunity(
    List<Opportunity> newlist,
    Map<ID, Opportunity> newmap)
    {
        if(AssociateContacts!=null)
            CreateSomeContactRoles(newlist,
            AssociateContacts);

        List<OpportunityContactRole> ocrs =
        [SELECT ID, ContactID, IsPrimary,
        OpportunityID from OpportunityContactRole
        where OpportunityID in :newmap.keyset()];

        Set<ID> OcrOpportunities = new Set<ID>();

        for(OpportunityContactRole ocr: ocrs)
            OcrOpportunities.add(ocr.OpportunityID);

        for(Opportunity op: newlist)
        {
            if(! OcrOpportunities.contains(op.id))
            op.addError('Opportunity Contact Role is
            required to create an opportunity');
        }

        // Other functionality
    }
}

private static void CreateSomeContactRoles(
    List<Opportunity> ops, List<Contact> cts)
    {
        List<OpportunityContactRole> newocrs =
            new List<OpportunityContactRole>();
```

```
    for(Integer x = 0; x< ops.size(); x++)
    {
        newocrs.add(
            new OpportunityContactRole(
            OpportunityID = ops[x].id,
            ContactID = cts[x].id,
            IsPrimary = true));
    }
    insert newocrs;

}
```

Modify the test code to the following:

```
static testMethod void test3()
{
    Opportunity op = new Opportunity(
        name='optest', StageName ='Prospecting',
        CloseDate = Date.Today() );

    Contact ct = new Contact(LastName = 'newct');
    insert ct;
    ThinkingInApex.AssociateContacts =
        new List<Contact>{ct};

    insert op;
}
```

The test code loads the ThinkingInApex.AssociateContacts static variable with the contacts to use when creating OpportunityContactRole objects for testing purposes. This design pattern turns out to be useful for implementing a variety of test scenarios that would otherwise be impossible.

By the way, do you see now why I implemented the trigger code in a class instead of a trigger? You can't add static variables to a trigger. It's true that I could have used a static variable in another class (though not a test class) and accessed it from the trigger, but this approach is cleaner and easier to follow and maintain. This is just one of the reasons why you should always minimize the amount of code in a trigger, and instead implement all functionality in a class. You'll see additional reasons later in this book.

As you have seen, the unique nature of static variables under Apex makes them an essential part of many Apex design patterns. Now let's take a look at the next key concept that fills the thoughts (and nightmares) of every Apex programmer. It's time to look at limits.

3 – Limits

You are almost certainly aware that the Force.com platform is a pioneer in the area of cloud computing. And, if you've been exposed to any technical, marketing or investor related media, you've undoubtedly heard that cloud computing is the latest and greatest thing (next to, perhaps, mobile and social networking). But cloud computing means different things to different people.

Everyone agrees on the fundamental idea of cloud computing. Instead of deploying applications and managing them on millions of client computers, run the applications on a redundant "cloud" of server machines, and access those resources through the Internet.

The advantages of such an approach are clear:

- Instead of having to update and maintain software on numerous client machines, you can do so on a relatively few server machines. This reduces the need to build up IT infrastructure and knowledge at each client site.
- Client machines typically don't use a fraction of their computing power – which wastes energy and resources. Sharing powerful server resources is much more efficient.

But the second point raises another issue. While client machines are rarely used to their full capability, that capability is there if needed. If a programming mistake or particular problem or requirement demands intensive computer resources – the drain caused by that mistake, problem or requirement is limited to that one client machine.

On the cloud, where servers are shared among many clients, how do you deal with those situations that suddenly demand a huge amount of resources?

One approach, used by cloud systems such as Amazon.com, is to provide users with virtual machines that have a specified limit on computational resources (memory, CPU speed, etc.). If you need more resources, you can purchase them as needed.

The Force.com platform took a different approach as befits its' different architecture. To protect the cloud from having any one bug, problem or requirement tie up too many resources, monitoring was built-in to the underlying application programming language to prevent applications from exceeding certain limits.

In a way, the choice of the word "limits" is unfortunate. After all, no programmer wants to feel limited by his or her tools. Yet the reality is that we are always working with limits of some sort – be it memory, or stack depth, or available language or platform features. It's just that over the past decade or two, thanks to Moore's law, the amount of computational power on the typical PC is far greater than most software developers really need. It wasn't that long ago that developers struggled to cram complex applications into 64K of memory. Some software developers do deal with limits on a regular basis – game developers are always trading off graphic quality against available hardware. Mobile developers have numerous platform limits to deal with. But even there, hardware continues to rapidly extend those limits.

So it's not that Apex limits are inherently bad. It's just that they are different and unfamiliar to most developers. Like any limits, their existence has a profound impact on architecture and design patterns. Once you become familiar with those limits, and the design patterns they require, you will find that limits are not only easy to deal with, they are part of what makes Apex programming fun. And you'll find that you have become a better programmer along the way.

I am not going to try to cover all of the limits here, or to list current limits. Limits often change between releases, so you should be referencing the platform documentation for that information. But I will discuss the limits that most often cause problems, and how you can trade off one against another.

The Nature of Limits

There is a trick when looking at limits in Apex. Don't focus on the values that you aren't supposed to exceed. Instead, consider each limit a pointer to an operation that you want to optimize throughout your code.

There are two reasons for taking this approach:

- If you focus on optimizing all of your limit related code, in many cases you will never come close to using the available limits.

- Remember that your code may not be the only code running in an execution context or organization. There may already be existing code in an organization. Some other developer may add other triggers after you are no longer around. If you are creating a package, there may be other packages installed that might be sharing some limits. If you focus on minimizing your own resource use, you are much more likely to avoid conflicts with other code.

There are many types of limits in the Force.com platform, depending on your edition and the platform features you have purchased. For our purposes, we will only concern ourselves with the Force.com platform limits – those that relate to Apex code. A complete and current list of limits can be found on the developer.force.com site.

Apex governor limits fall into several categories:

- Limits that apply to a single execution context, regardless of packaging.
- Limits that apply to a single execution context, where each package has its own set of limits.
- Limits that apply to a 24 hour period for an organization.

For most developers, the first two categories will actually be the same. All of the Apex code on your system will share one set of limits. There are two exceptions to this. The first, and most important, is that when creating unit tests, you have one set of limits for test initialization and validation, and another for running the test itself (the code between the StartTest and StopTest methods – you'll read more about this in chapter 10). The other exception relates to managed packages that are listed on the AppExchange by Salesforce.com ISV partners. These packages can receive their own set of governor limits within an execution context. This is important both for users – who can install packages with less worry that they will cause existing code to start failing due to Apex limits, and for package developers, who can be more confident that their packages will not fail due to limits caused by other packages or custom code on an organization.

Dealing with Limits

The type of application you are building will determine which limits concern you most. In most cases, you can, through careful design, trade off one limit against another to avoid problems. Let's take a look at the most important limits, and common ways to deal with them.

SOQL Queries

This limit was extraordinarily painful back in the days when you were limited to a small number of SOQL queries in an execution context. Now, it's unlikely that well written code will ever come close to this limit. The trick is to make sure that your code is well written:

- Always use bulk syntax (see Bulk Patterns later in this chapter).
- Use before-triggers instead of after-triggers where possible (allows modification of fields without a SOQL query and DML update).
- Cache query results if your design allows.
- Include fields from related objects in a single query.

Let's take a closer look at the last one.

Consider the scenario where you want to query a set of contacts and, as part of the functionality, make sure that if any of those contacts belongs to an account, the account has an AnnualRevenue forecast set.

Your first thought, especially if you are extending existing code, might be to build a list of the account IDs and query for those accounts thus:

```
// Query for contact info
List<Contact> cts = [SELECT ID, AccountID
        from Contact where your condition here];

// Some code that operates on the contacts here....

// Get list of account IDs.
Set<ID> accountids = new Set<ID>();
for(Contact ct: cts) if(ct.AccountID!=null)
```

```
        accountids.add(ct.AccountID);

if(accountids.size()>0)
{
    List<Account> accounts = [Select ID, AnnualRevenue
            from Account where ID in :accountids];
    for(Account accountfound: accounts)
        if(accountfound.AnnualRevenue == null)
            accountfound.AnnualRevenue = 500;
    update accounts;
    }
}
```

This is a perfectly reasonable implementation that uses two SOQL queries. It's particularly nice if you are extending code that has an existing contact query, as it minimizes impact on existing code.

But the following approach works well also:

```
// Query for contact info and annual revenue on
// account in a single query

List<Contact> cts = [SELECT ID, AccountID,
    Account.ID, Account.AnnualRevenue from
    Contact where your condition here];

// Some code that operates on the contacts here....

Map<ID, Account> accountstoupdate =
                    new Map<ID,Account>();

for(Contact ct: cts)
{
    if (ct.Account.AnnualRevenue == null)
    {
        ct.Account.AnnualRevenue = 500;
```

```
        accountstoupdate.put(ct.AccountID, ct.Account);
    }
}
        update accountstoupdate.values();
```

This code is a bit trickier in that you need to pull the account objects out of the contact list in order to do the update (updating the contact list won't update any referenced objects). The code uses a map to do this instead of a list, because of the possibility that multiple contacts will reference the same account.

This approach uses about the same amount of memory and script statements as the first, but only requires one SOQL statement.

CPU Time Limits/Script Statements

Before the Winter 2014 release, SFDC enforced a limit of 200,000 script statements in a synchronous execution context. That sounds like a lot until you remember that in most cases your code needs to be able to handle batches of 200 records at a time. That would leave you 1000 script statements per record – which is still a generous number in most cases.

But when you realize that a single SOQL query can retrieve up to 50,000 records, it quickly becomes apparent that any query returning that many records is virtually useless in a standard execution contact, as you can't do very much with a record with only 4 lines of code.

Using the SOQL loop syntax to break the query into blocks of 200 doesn't help – as that doesn't give you additional script lines to work with.

Effective Winter 2014, Salesforce began the transition away from script limits in favor of a single global CPU limit per transaction –

10 seconds for synchronous code and 60 seconds for asynchronous code.

This change from script limits to CPU time limits has several major impacts on Apex development:

- CPU time limits include time spent on built-in functions. For example: where before a call to the built-in array sort function would cost only one script statement, it now costs whatever CPU time is used to do the sort.

- CPU time limits include other operations, such as workflows and formula calculations, that were previously not included in governor limits. CPU time limits do not include time spent performing database operations and queries, or waiting on responses from callouts.

- CPU time limits are global to all running code. In other words, each managed package does not get its own CPU time limit.

What does this change mean in practice?

For most developers, it does represent a relaxing of limits. While it is difficult to accurately measure the CPU time required by different operations, it is possible to do some rough benchmarking to get a general idea of how long they take. Simple operations such as assignments, simple math operations, and function calls, typically run in under 1 microsecond. Collection operations come in at about 3 microseconds. Even if you assumed that other longer operations would increase your average script time to 5 microseconds, the 10 second synchronous limit would translate into two million script lines – a significant increase over the previous 200,000 script line limit.

But there are two major flaws to this calculation.

First, the previous set of script limits was not 200,000 per synchronous execution context, but 200,000 for each AppExchange managed package running in that context. Because your code could access up to 10 managed packages in one context, the theoretical script limit was actually 1.2 million script lines (200,000 per package and another 200,000 for code native to the organization).

Second, this calculation does not factor in workflows, formulas, and built-in functions that can take much longer to run. To use some extreme examples: Deep cloning an array of 100 SObjects with 8 fields each takes about 25 milliseconds. You could fit 400 of those operations into a ten second CPU time limit. Performing a JSON serialization operation on an array of 20,000 integers takes about 1/3 of a second, meaning you could fit all of 30 of those operations into a synchronous execution context.

Built-in Salesforce methods that operate on large amounts of data, such as sorting and serialization, now cost their full CPU time, where before they only counted as a single script statement.

With these facts in mind, the change from script limits to CPU limits has a number of direct impacts on Apex development best practices:

- The need to optimize your code remains, and in some ways is even greater than before, especially if you are developing a managed package. It is now possible for one greedy package to use more than its fair share of CPU time, or for excessive CPU time use in organization code to cause packages to fail. Ideally, you should design your code to never use more than 1/10 of the available CPU time, and perform bulk testing to verify this under worst-case conditions.

- Estimating the limit cost of code during the design phase is somewhat trickier than before – as you must weigh in the differing costs of different operations.

- There are a number of common code optimization techniques used prior to the Winter 14 release that are no longer applicable: Previously, all elements in a conditional statement were counted as a single script line. As a result, it was common to create very large and complex conditional statements, resulting in code that was efficient, but difficult to read and understand. There is no longer any benefit in taking this approach, so Apex developers can feel free to break them up into multiple conditional statements that are easier to understand and maintain.

  For example: where before you might code:

```
if( (A && B && !C)  || (D && E) || (F && G) ) dosomething();
```

  You can now use:

```
Boolean doOperation = false;
if(A && B && !C) doOperation = true;
if (D && E) doOperation = true;
if( F && G) doOperation = true;
if(doOperation) dosomething();
```

  Where before the latter approach could have potentially increased your script count from one to five, now the increase is negligible, perhaps 1 microsecond in CPU time.

- Previously, if you had a loop, there was a strong incentive to perform operations inline instead of implementing those operations as separate functions, as even saving the one or two script lines involved in making a function call could result in a huge savings in a large loop. There is no longer a reason to do this, as function calls in Apex are very efficient.

- Previously, you could sometimes move expressions or calculations into formulas or workflows, effectively getting that functionality for free in terms of script limits. Formulas and workflows are now included in CPU time calculations. There may still be good reasons to implement functionality in formulas and workflows – Apex should generally be the last resort (except when creating managed packages), but the decision should be driven by other considerations – not limits.

There are a number of things you can do if you find yourself running up against CPU time limits:

- Move your code to a future call. Future calls have, and probably will always have, larger limits than trigger execution contexts. One common design pattern is to use a custom field on an object to indicate that an operation is pending, then to query on that flag during a future operation. Another approach is to use a custom object that you create to hold all of the information needed to perform the future operation, then just query for instances of that object (deleting them after the operation is complete).

- Move your code into batch Apex. This is the preferred design pattern when dealing with large data sets.

- Optimize your code. You'll see various examples of code optimization throughout the rest of this book.

Benchmarking

It has always been important to measure the performance of Apex code in order to determine where you should invest the most effort with regards to optimizing your code. With the advent of CPU time limits, it is important to know how to measure not just the performance of your code, but also the performance of built-in Salesforce functionality.

Mark Twain has often been misquoted as saying: "There lies, damned lies, and computer software benchmarks". Yes, I know – he was referring to statistics. But I'm confident that if he had lived to see computers, he would have quickly realized that when it comes to misinterpretation and manipulation of results, software benchmarks are the worst kind of statistics.

Despite this, it is possible to use a few simple techniques to estimate the performance of a given built-in function. The trick is to place the operation you want to measure inside of a loop, perform the operation multiple times, then divide the time spent by the number of iterations.

For example, let's say you want to measure the time it takes to allocate a new Map collection. Using the developer console, set the log levels to INFO or WARNING for Apex Code and System – you're going to be running many operations and don't want to load all that data into your debug log. Set the profiling level to FINEST.

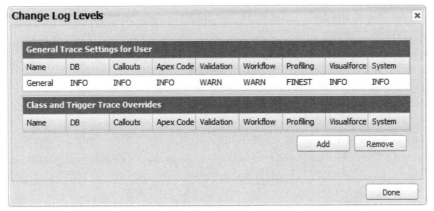

Figure 3-1 – Log level setting in the developer console

Your benchmarking code framework might look something like this:

```
@isTest
private class Benchmarking {

    @istest
    public static void TestNewAllocate()
    {
        for(Integer x = 0; x<10000; x++)
            ReturnNewMap();
    }

    private static Map<Integer,String> ReturnNewMap()
    {
        Map<Integer,String> result = new Map<Integer,String>();
        return result;
    }
}
```

When you look at the resulting execution log, there are two numbers to look for. Maximum CPU time in the limits section:

13:33:31:000 LIMIT_USAGE_FOR_NS   Maximum CPU time: 0
out of 10000

And the CUMULATIVE_PROFILING time in the profiling section
for the ReturnNewMap function:

```
18:24:52:000 CUMULATIVE_PROFILING
Class.TestCPUTimes.TestNewAllocate: line 9, column 1: private
static MAP<Integer,String> ReturnNewMap(): executed 10000 times
in 46 ms
```

What this tells us is that the 10000 iteration loop wasn't really
enough for the debug log to even report back the CPU time, but we
do have a sense of the elapsed time in the ReturnNewMap function. Because there are no database operations or callouts in the
function, the elapsed time can be used to represent the CPU time
(which is certain to always be less than the elapsed time).

The profile information tells us that 10,000 map allocations takes
no more than 46 milliseconds. Thus a single map allocation takes
no more than 4.6 microseconds (46ms/10000 = 0.0046ms = 4.6
us).

There are some subtle aspects to this approach. Why not place the
allocation inside of the loop? Why call a function?

The reason is that the Apex compiler is an optimizing compiler. If
it sees that you are calling a function that doesn't do anything, it
may not call the function. If it sees you allocating a collection that
you don't use, it may choose to skip allocating the collection. The
approach shown here is designed to at least try to trick the system
into actually running the code. We know the ReturnNewMap function is called because the profiler tells us so.

Another approach would have been to use a much larger loop –
large enough for the CPU time limits to start showing up. You

would expect the CPU time to be less than the elapsed time – sometimes considerably less. While using a larger loop does sound good in theory, in practice the profiling data tends to be more consistent and repeatable than the CPU time totals. Plus, it allows you to focus on specific lines of code.

Keep in mind that the purpose of benchmarking here is not to accurately measure the performance of the code – it is to estimate the worst case cost of a built-in function. In this case, you can have high confidence that the cost to allocate a new map is about 5 microseconds, which is slightly longer than the simplest operations.

What this tells you in practice is that you don't need to pay any special attention to map allocation – when estimating performance you can treat it as an ordinary low-impact line of code.

Now, let's look at a higher impact statement. Consider this test code:

```
@istest
public static void TestSorts()
{
    List<Integer> unsorteddata = new List<Integer>();
    for(Integer x = 0; x<500; x++)
    {
        unsorteddata.add(x); unsorteddata.add(x+500);
    }
    for(Integer x = 0; x< 10000; x++)
    {
        ReturnSorted(unsorteddata);
    }

}
private static List<Integer> ReturnSorted(
                List<Integer> inputlist)
```

```
{
    List<Integer> sortedlist1 = inputlist.clone();
    sortedlist1.sort();
    return sortedlist1;
}
```

Here we're allocating an array of 1000 unsorted integers, and sorting it 10,000 times. This is an arbitrary set of data – for a more in-depth analysis you would likely want to initialize the array with a variety of data sets to gain an understanding of possible worst case scenarios.

Because we're doing fine profiling, we can again look at the exact line that's making this call:

```
14:10:22:000 CUMULATIVE_PROFILING
Class.TestCPUTimes.ReturnSorted: line 38, column 1: global
public void sort(): executed 10000 times in 2881 ms
```

As a longer operation, you should see the CPU time appear in the limits as well. Because the CPU time includes all of the time used in your code, it may well be larger than the number returned by the profiler for that particular line of code.

What does this tell us? Sorting an array with 1000 numbers in this case is taking 2881/10000 = 0.28 milliseconds. It's still a fairly small number, but if you are trying to keep all of your code under 1 second of CPU time (1/10 of the ten second synchronous limit), that single sort function took up 0.28% of your available time. It's certainly not the kind of operation you would want to put inside of a loop.

Let me again stress that this kind of benchmarking is very rough. If the server your organization is on is very busy, the elapsed time can significantly exceed the CPU time. You should always run multiple tests, as timing (even CPU timing) can vary between runs. The goal here is not to accurately measure the performance of your code, but to come up with reasonable and conservative estimates that you can use to understand how certain design choices may impact performance. You'll see how this works in the next chapter.

Other Limits

Here is a brief list of some of the other key limits and some common tradeoffs you can use with each one.

DML Limits

There is a limit to the number of DML (Database) operations you can perform within an execution context.

- Combine DML operations on each object type into a single bulk DML operation.
- If your program flow calls for DML operations at different places in your code, don't perform the DML operation right away. Instead, store a reference to the object in a list, set or Map. Then perform a DML operation on all objects at once as the last part of your operation. You'll see examples of this approach in chapter 6.

Heap Size

The size of the heap is limited during an execution context.

- When performing SOQL queries, only include fields you actually need in the query. In particular, avoid querying for long text and rich text fields.
- Instead of storing objects in a static variable, store Object IDs, then requery when needed.

Describes

Describe calls allow you to obtain information about Force.com objects and fields.

- Use static variables to cache describe information so that no more than one call is made for each SObject type or field during an execution context.
- Don't use Describe functions to obtain fixed information on standard fields and objects. For example: standard field data types don't change – so hardcode that data to avoid a Describe call.
- If necessary, cache describe data in a custom object which you can then query later. Use XML or JSON serialization to store all of the data you need in a single object field, allowing one SOQL query to replace multiple describe calls.

Callouts

Apex code can call out to external web services. There is a limit to the number of callouts in an execution context.

- Don't try using callouts in a trigger context – it's not supported.
- On a Visual Force page, you can often extend your limits by placing content in an Iframe. Each Iframe runs in its own execution context.

API Limits

You can implement API entry points in Apex that allow outside applications to call in to your code. Each API request generates its own execution context. The number of allowed API requests is limited for each organization over a 24 hour period.

- Always support bulk operations for every API call. This can reduce the number of incoming calls.

- Specify a limit to the amount of data in each call, or set an "out" parameter to specify that additional data is available in cases where you can't serve up all the data requested. This will allow you to dynamically adjust the tradeoff between the limit on the number of API calls and the limit on data that can be transferred on each call.

Email Limits

You are limited in the number of external Email you can send, both in terms of number of Emails and number of recipients.

- When sending Email to internal users with Apex code, specify the destination using their UserID, not their Email address. These Emails are not subject to limits.

Thinking of Limits

This part of the book is all about thinking in Apex. There's a tendency, when coming to Apex from other languages, to think of it as a familiar language, where limits are just one of those quirky things to consider when programming, just as every other platform has its little quirks. Then one day, when you run up against those limits, they suddenly become an annoying obstacle, and you find yourself cursing Salesforce.com for building them into the system and getting in your way, even though you intellectually understand why they are there. That was certainly my experience when starting out.

My hope, with this book, is to change the way you look at limits. To accept (if not embrace them) as a fundamental part of the platform, and one that has as great an impact on software design and architecture as any other language or platform feature. Once you start seeing limits as a top level factor to incorporate into your design and architecture from day one, you'll find that in most cases limits become easy to deal with. You'll be able to choose effective tradeoffs between various limits during project design, and even build your code to detect when it is approaching limits during execution, and automatically defer operations as necessary into future or batch Apex calls.

In no time, limits will become just another minor issue to deal with. You'll be writing good code from the start, and will only rarely find yourself needing to go back and resolve limit issues.

4 – Bulk Patterns

One of the first things that every Apex programmer learns is that Apex programming has certain bulk patterns. Everyone knows that triggers can receive up to 200 objects at once. Everyone knows that SOQL queries and DML statements should not be inside of loops. The documentation on the importance of bulk patterns is clear, and not easy to miss.

Yet despite this, there's a trap that almost every beginning Apex programmer falls into, especially those coming from another language. They design and create code that is intended to work on one object at a time, and then figure out ways to "bulkify" it afterwards. In my own consulting work, I've been astonished how often I've run into triggers that are sure to fail the instant anyone does a bulk upload or update.

In this chapter, we'll walk through a number of bulk patterns and scenarios. But before we start, here's the most important thing for you to remember and follow.

> **All of your Apex code should be designed to handle bulk operations.**
> **All of it – no exceptions.**

If you're an experienced Apex programmer, you're probably thinking: "wait a minute – there are times when bulk coding really isn't necessary. VisualForce controllers often work on single objects. Queries that return one object either by design or a LIMIT=1 qualifier don't need bulk patterns. What are you thinking?"

Hear me out.

Bulk patterns and single object patterns, as you will see, are very different. It's true that sometimes bulkifying code is a simple matter of storing values in a collection that will be used for a bulk DML or query later. But if you design with bulk data in mind, you can often come up with far more efficient solutions.

In other words, you will end up with better code if you design your code with bulk patterns from the start, than if you write it for single objects and try to convert it later. You'll also spend less time, as you won't have to rewrite and redesign your code.

In Apex, bulk patterns are far more common than single object patterns. So common that there is actually little reason to learn the single object patterns at all. If you use bulk patterns everywhere, you'll maintain a higher level of code consistency (which will improve the maintainability of your code), and reduce your learning curve. If you commit to using bulk patterns everywhere from the beginning, it will encourage (even force) you to learn them – instead of falling back on the single object patterns that you already know from other platforms.

Most books or articles at this point would demonstrate a variety of patterns using simple examples. However, as it is my hope to help you learn to think in Apex, and since this is a book intended for advanced developers (or those who wish to become advanced developers), let's take a journey through a more complex example.

Note – I strongly recommend that you install the sample code, uncomment the relevant samples, and be prepared to examine them and experiment with them. Some of the code in this chapter is more advanced than you would see in a typical book or article.

An Interesting Challenge

In Salesforce, every sales opportunity (defined by the Opportunity object) can have one or more contacts associated it. This association is defined using an OpportunityContactRole object, which includes a ContactID, OpportunityID and IsPrimary field. This IsPrimary field determines if this is the primary contact for the opportunity, of which there can only be one.

Consider the business case where you wish to guarantee that your opportunity always has a primary contact. If it doesn't, you want to assign one.

This may sound simple, but it's actually quite a challenge.

- The only time Salesforce automatically assigns a primary contact is when you create an opportunity from the contact page.
- When you create an opportunity during lead conversion, Salesforce does create an OpportunityContactRole for the contact on the opportunity, but it isn't primary.
- You could use UI techniques to make sure users only create opportunities from the contact page, but that won't help with opportunities created though external tools (API, data import, Apex, etc.)

This is exactly the kind of problem that often lands in the hands of an Apex developer. Your first thoughts might include using a trigger on the OpportunityContactRole object and performing any necessary validation when one is created or deleted. However, Salesforce does not support triggers on the OpportunityContactRole object.

So there is no perfect solution to the problem.

That means it's necessary to go back and figure out what the sales or marketing team really needs (which isn't always what they ask for).

Let's assume that, for our scenario, after extensive discussion with all of the stakeholders, it is determined that a good solution would be to make sure that a primary contact is assigned before the opportunity stage can be changed. This actually makes a certain amount of business sense, as it allows the sales team to create opportunities, but ensures that a primary contact is assigned before the opportunity moves to the next stage in the sales cycle.

To make life easier on the sales team, they want you to add some logic to automatically assign an existing contact as the primary contact based on the following logic:

- Contacts are often associated with multiple opportunities. Whichever contact is a primary contact on the most opportunities should be chosen as primary.
- If there is a tie on the above criteria, whichever contact is associated with the most opportunities (primary or not) should be chosen as primary.
- If there is a tie, choose an arbitrary contact to be primary.
- If there are no related contacts on an opportunity, create a task for the opportunity owner (if a task doesn't already exist).

This is based on the idea that the contact who is involved in the most opportunities would be the most likely contact on new opportunities.

Those are the requirements. You may be tempted to start coding right away, but doing so will likely lead you astray. Not only is there some serious design work to be done, but as is often the case with Apex, there is some testing to do as well.

Building to Tests

Testing in Apex is a very complex subject that I'll be covering in depth later. But it's worth bringing up here for a number of reasons:

- It's not exactly clear at this point how to implement the requirements we've defined. However, as you will see, implementing tests for those requirements is quite straightforward.
- Bulk patterns apply to unit tests as well as other Apex code modules. You need bulk tests to test bulk code. So test code is as good a place to start demonstrating bulk patterns as anywhere.
- You'll be seeing several different solutions to this challenge. Having a unit test in place makes it easy to compare the performance and resource use of the various implementations.

The Force.com platform is unusual in that it requires unit tests in order to deploy code to production. Since tests are required, there is no reason not to write them first if the requirements are reasonably clear. In fact, some developers subscribe to test-driven design methodologies that require you to create tests before implementation code.

For the time being, let's limit ourselves to a couple of simple tests that validate functionality. The goal is to obtain a simple yes/no answer – does the code work? Other goals, such as obtaining code coverage, handling invalid input, and so forth, are secondary – those are subjects we'll cover in Chapter 10.

The basic flow of the tests is simple:

- Create one or more contacts.
- Create one or more opportunities.
- Create non-primary contact roles to associate those contacts with the opportunities.
- Update the stage for one or more of the opportunities.

- Verify that each updated opportunity has a primary contact.

As you can see, the basic functional test is much simpler than scenario we need to implement. This isn't always the case.

This flow leaves some questions open. How many contacts should be created? How many opportunities? How do we handle opportunities whose stages are not being updated?

One common design pattern is to create utility functions that can be shared by multiple test classes or methods. In this example, there are two utility functions. The first one, TestBulkPatterns.InitTestObjects, sets up the test scenario based on some parameters. The newopportunities parameter references a list that is initialized by this function with the new opportunities. NumberOfOpportunities specifies the number of new opportunities to create. NumberOfOtherOpportunties specifies the number of additional opportunities to create – opportunities that will be associated with the contacts, but will not be updated by the test code. ContactRolesPerOp specifies the number of contacts to be associated with each opportunity. NumberOfContacts specifies the number of contacts to distribute among the opportunities, and is required to be at larger or equal to ContactRolesPerOp.

```
// Prepare the specified number of opportunities,
// with contact roles on each.
// The contact roles are distributed evenly among
// the number of contacts specified.
    public static void InitTestObjects(
    List<Opportunity> newopportunities,
    Integer NumberOfOpportunities, Integer
    NumberOfOtherOpportunities, Integer
    ContactRolesPerOp, Integer NumberOfContacts)
{

    if(NumberOfContacts < ContactRolesPerOp)
```

```
    NumberOfContacts = ContactRolesPerOp;

List<Contact>cts = new List<Contact>();
for(Integer x=0;x<numberofcontacts;x++)
{
    cts.add(new Contact(LastName = 'cttest_' +
    String.valueOf(x)));
}

insert cts;
```

The code for creating contacts and opportunities shows a common test pattern to create a specified number of objects with different names or other field values.

```
newopportunities.clear();
for(Integer x=0; x<NumberOfOpportunities; x++)
{
    newopportunities.add(new Opportunity(CloseDate
    = Date.Today().addDays(5), Name = 'optest_' +
    String.valueOf(x),
    StageName = 'Prospecting' ));
}

// Insert the test opportunities
insert newopportunities;

List<Opportunity> otheropportunities =
    new List<Opportunity>();
for(Integer x=0; x<NumberOfOtherOpportunities;
    x++)
{
    otheropportunities.add(new Opportunity(
        CloseDate = Date.Today().addDays(5),
        Name = 'optest_' + String.valueOf(x +
        NumberOfOpportunities),
```

```
            StageName = 'Prospecting' ));
    }
    insert otheropportunities;
    otheropportunities.addall(newopportunities);
    // Combine the two for creating
    // OpportunityContactRoles

    // Now insert contact roles
    List<OpportunityContactRole> ocrlist =
            new List<OpportunityContactRole>();
    Integer contactnumber = 0;
    for(Opportunity op: otheropportunities)
    {
        for(Integer ocrnumber = 0;
            ocrnumber < ContactRolesPerOp; ocrnumber++)
        {
            ocrlist.add(new OpportunityContactRole(
                OpportunityID = op.id,
                ContactID = cts[contactnumber].id));
            contactnumber++;
            if(contactnumber >= NumberOfContacts)
                contactnumber = 0;
        }

    }
    insert ocrlist;
}
```

The next utility function takes a list of Opportunity objects, and makes sure that each one has one primary contact.

```
public static void ValidateOCRs(List<Opportunity> ops)
{
    // Get map for IDs
    Map<ID, Opportunity> opmap = new Map<ID, Opportunity>(ops);
```

```
// Query for primary Contacts
List<OpportunityContactRole> ocrs =
[SELECT ID from OpportunityContactRole
where OpportunityID in :opmap.keyset() And IsPrimary= true];

// Create set of opportunity IDs with primary contacts
Set<ID> OpportunitiesWithPrimaryContact = new Set<ID>();
for(OpportunityContactRole ocr: ocrs)
    OpportunitiesWithPrimaryContact.add(ocr.OpportunityID);

// Now make sure every opportunity has a primary contact role
for(Opportunity op: ops)
    System.Assert(
        OpportunitiesWithPrimaryContact.contains(op.id));
}
```

Unit tests are unique in that they have two sets of governor limits available: one set used for setting up data and verifying results, and one set for the test itself (the code between a call to the Test.StartTest and Test.StopTest methods). You'll typically call the ValidateOCRs function after calling Test.StopTest so it will be in the non-testing set of limits. Even so, it's best to write the setup and verification code to be as efficient as possible. Here's a demonstration of how use of an Apex subquery can eliminate a loop. You'll see later how valuable this technique can be.

```
public static void ValidateOCRs(
    List<Opportunity> ops)
{
    // Get map for IDs
    Map<ID, Opportunity> opmap = new Map<ID, Opportunity>(ops);

    List<Opportunity> opresults = [SELECT ID,
        (SELECT ID from OpportunityContactRoles
        where IsPrimary = true) from opportunity
```

```
        where ID in :opmap.keyset() ];
    for(Opportunity op: opresults)
        System.Assert( op.OpportunityContactRoles.size()==1);
}
```

With these utility functions in place, the tests themselves are easy to write. First, the BulkOpportunityTest demonstrates how to tie the utility functions together into a functional test:

```
static testMethod void BulkOpportunityTest() {
    List<Opportunity> ops = new List<Opportunity>();
    InitTestObjects(ops, 100, 20, 20, 40);

    Test.StartTest();
    for(Opportunity op: ops)
        op.StageName = 'Qualification';
    update ops;
    Test.StopTest();

    ValidateOCRs(ops);
}
```

You can get different test behaviors, and test different limits, by choosing different parameters to InitTestObjects. You can also create several different tests that use different parameters, reducing the amount of code needed to implement your complete set of unit tests.

The BulkOpportunity test and utility functions validate the part of the requirements that ensures that a primary contact exists for opportunities that are already associated with contacts. But it doesn't test the condition where there are no contacts associated with an opportunity. The TestBulkPatterns.CreateTaskTest verifies that part of the functionality.

```
@istest(oninstall=true seealldata=false)
static void CreateTaskTest()
{
    Integer NumberOfOpportunities = 100;
    List<Opportunity> ops = new List<Opportunity>();
    for(Integer x=0; x<NumberOfOpportunities; x++)
    {
        ops.add(new Opportunity(
        CloseDate = Date.Today().addDays(5),
        Name = 'optest_' + String.valueOf(x),
        StageName = 'Prospecting' ));
    }
    insert ops;

    Test.StartTest();
    for(Opportunity op: ops)
        op.StageName = 'Qualification';
    update ops;
    Test.StopTest();

    List<Task> tasks = [SELECT ID, OwnerID,
    WhatID, Status, Subject, Type from Task
    where OwnerID = :UserInfo.getUserID()
    And Type='Other' And IsClosed = False And
    Subject = 'Assign Primary Contact'   ];

    system.assertEquals(NumberOfOpportunities,
    tasks.size());
}
```

This test poses an interesting challenge. How do you ensure that the tasks being queried during the validation are those that were created during this execution context? This can certainly be a problem when running the test on a production system.

- You could look at the task creation time and make sure the task was created after the test started running. This would be fine, unless someone just happened to update an opportunity and create a task while the test was running.
- You could modify the code to store a list of newly created task IDs in a static variable. Because the unit test code shares the same execution context as the code being tested, it could grab the list of newly created tasks and query only those tasks.
- This example chose a third approach. By setting the seealldata=false option, only those tasks created during this execution context are visible to the unit test.

Ok, you got me. This was a trick question.

As of API version 24, seealldata=false is the default setting for test classes. So this issue would never come up - unless, of course, you are writing to an older version of the API (which can happen, as you will see in the chapter on Packaging).

Evaluating Worst-Case Conditions

When designing code for bulk processing, it is important to evaluate the worst-case scenario for every part of the implementation. This starts with understanding the size of the data input. For triggers, this is generally 200 objects at a time.

Let's do a worst case assessment of a very simple, non bulkified, translation of the requirements into pseudocode[1].

---

[1] Pseudocode, for those who are not familiar with the concept, is a way of describing software functionality without using the syntax of any particular language.

```
Look for a change in opportunity status
If the opportunity has no OpportunityContactRole objects, check
if a task to create a primary contact already exists.
    If it does, exit.
    If not, create the task and then exit.
Are any of the OpportunityContractRole objects primary?
    If so, exit.
    If not, get a list of the contacts associated
    with the opportunity.
    Query all of the OpportunityContactRole objects
    associated with those contacts.
    For each contact
        Count the number of primary
        OpportunityContactRole objects.
        Count the total number of
        OpportunityContactRole objects.
        Keep track of which contact best matches the
        criteria (most primary, then best total if
        primaries are equal).
    Find the the best qualifying contact, and set
    the original OpportunityContactRole for that
    contact to primary.
```

What happens if 200 opportunities are updated at once?

If this algorithm were implemented within a loop that enumerates those opportunities, everything in the algorithm could happen up to 200 times.

Let's look at this algorithm again:

```
Look for a change in opportunity status
If the opportunity has no OpportunityContactRole objects, check
if a task to create a primary contact already exists.
    If it does, exit
    If not, create the task and then exit.
```

That's a query for OpportunityContactRole objects.

In a worst case scenario, this results in up to one query for existing Task objects and one DML operation to insert a new Task object.

```
Are any of the OpportunityContractRole objects primary?
```

How many OpportunityContactRole objects might be on an opportunity? It really depends on the type of organization and business. There's no theoretical upper limit, so you need to choose a realistic worst case – a worst case number that should work for any real organization. Let's assume that even the largest B2B organization won't exceed an average of 20 contacts per opportunity. So this test has a worst case of 20 loop iterations.

```
If so, exit
If not, get a list of the contacts associated
with the opportunity.
```

Building the list of contact IDs is another 20 loop iterations.

```
Query all of the OpportunityContactRole objects
associated with those contacts.
```

How many opportunities might a given contact be involved in? Again, there's no theoretical maximum, so we need to come up with a realistic worst case. Let's say that as a worse case an average contact could be involved with 100 opportunities. So this would be a query that returns 100 results for each of 20 contacts.

```
For each contact
    Count the number of primary
    OpportunityContactRole objects
    Count the total number of
    OpportunityContactRole objects
    Keep track of which contact best matches the
```

```
criteria (most primary, then best total if
primaries are equal)
```

This becomes a 100 iteration loop with several script lines.

```
Find the the best qualifying contact, and set
the original OpportunityContactRole for that
contact to primary.
```

This ends with a DML statement.

So to process a single opportunity, we have as worst cases:

- One Task Query + One DML operation

Or

- 2 x 20 iterations of about 2 script lines
- 1 Contact/OpportunityContactRole query @ 2000 records
- 20 x 100 iteration of a few script lines
- One DML operation

That seems easy enough, but what happens when you put it in a batch of 200 opportunities?

The task worst case becomes 200 queries or 200 DML operations – both exceed current limits.

The opportunity processing worst case becomes:

- 200 x 2 x 20 x 2 = 16,000 script lines
- 200 queries @ 400,000 records
- 200 x 20 x 100 x 3 = 1.2 million script lines
- 200 DML operations

Obviously, we have a problem. The number of queries and DML statements is something you probably expected and know how to deal with. If the functions called in the methods are simple, this will probably not exceed CPU time limits, though at 1.2 million script lines you can estimate the CPU time at about 2 seconds (figuring 1-2 microseconds per line), which is far more than the preferred target maximum of one second.

Unlike the queries and DML statements, the number or records queried and number of script lines is not easily reduced by just moving queries outside of a loop. These are issues that testing alone would not necessarily show, because the limits on unit tests prevent creation of very large numbers of records. Only incorporating a worst-case analysis as part of the design process allows you to anticipate these kinds of problems and be prepared to deal with them.

In the chapter on Limits, you learned that limit issues are generally addressed by trading off one limit against another. And indeed, the way you typically bulkify code with SOQL or DML operations inside of loops, is to use collections to prepare the necessary data and hold the results, moving the SOQL or DML out of the loop - trading additional script lines for a reduction in SOQL and DML operations.

But what do you do when you are already reaching limits on CPU time and number of records that can be retrieved by a query? How do you trade off one limit against another when your algorithm fails all limits in a worst-case scenario?

A Common Solution

Let's begin with a straightforward solution to the problem using common bulk design patterns. In the sample code, you'll see an implementation of the non-bulkified solution in class AfterUpdateOpportunityAwful – a solution so hopeless that I won't even bother including the whole thing here. The code we will look at is implemented in method AfterUpdateOpportunityCommon.

The method begins with a design pattern that is part of almost every bulk compatible trigger – a simple loop over the input data to identify which objects need to be processed.

```
public static void AfterUpdateOpportunityCommon(
    List<Opportunity> newlist, Map<ID, Opportunity>
    newmap, Map<ID, Opportunity> oldmap)
    {
        // Pattern 2 - Straightforward common
            implementation

        Set<ID> OpportunityIDsWithStagenameChanges =
                new Set<ID>();

        // Get OpportunityContactRoles
        for(Opportunity op: newlist)
        {
            if(op.StageName !=
                oldmap.get(op.id).StageName)
                OpportunityIDsWithStagenameChanges.add(op.id);
        }
        if(OpportunityIDsWithStagenameChanges.size()==0)
        return; // Quick exit if no processing required
```

In this case we build a set of IDs to the opportunities that have a stage change. We're not interested in any others. You'll see implementations of this pattern that use sets, lists and maps. It's really not critical which one you choose. The idea is to choose the one that captures the data that you actually need. In this case, the ID is sufficient because we already have a map (the newmap variable).

There is some very small saving in heap space by using a Set instead of a map – but it's a minor issue.

If you detect that no records need to be processed, exit the code as quickly as possible. This improves efficiency and reduces the chance of errors later in the code. There are some developers who feel strongly that every function should have a single exit point. If you prefer that approach, consider using a try/catch/finally block instead of complex nesting of conditional statements as shown in the following pseudocode.

```
function
    try
        Test condition
        If fail return

        continue operation
    catch
        rethrow error
    finally
        early return statement and any exceptions
        will all execute here
end function
```

The next step is to query all of the OpportunityContactRole objects related to these opportunities so we can evaluate if any opportunities already have primary contacts, or if any of them have no primary contacts.

```
// Query for all related OpportunityContactRole
List<OpportunityContactRole> ocrs = [Select ID,
    ContactID, IsPrimary, OpportunityID from
    OpportunityContactRole where OpportunityID in
    :OpportunityIDsWithStagenameChanges];
```

```
// Look for primary, or for no OCR on opportunities
Set<ID> primaryfound = new Set<ID>();
Set<ID> anyfound = new Set<ID>();

for(OpportunityContactRole ocr: ocrs)
{
    if(ocr.IsPrimary)
        primaryfound.add(ocr.OpportunityID);
        anyfound.add(ocr.OpportunityID);
}
```

As you recall, the worst case assessment of 20 OpportunityContactRole objects for each opportunity could result in 4000 records being retrieved here – so while this query is safe, we know there are potential problems. For this implementation, we're going to remain aware of these issues, but not incorporate them into the solution.

One question that arises is whether it might make sense to split this into two queries – one that pulls primary contacts (IsPrimary = true), and the other that doesn't. Doing so adds one query and might save a line or two of code at best – so while it is potentially a legitimate trade-off, it has such minor effect that it's not worth worrying about.

Now you have two sets, one that contains the IDs of all opportunities with primary contacts, the other that contains the IDs of all opportunities with any contacts.

```
// Build list of opportunities with no contact role,
// and list with contact role but no primary contact
// role
// Use maps because it's an easy way to get the
// keyset for later queries
Map<ID, Opportunity> OpsWithNoContactRoles =
```

```
        new Map<ID, Opportunity>();
Map<ID, Opportunity> OpsWithNoPrimary =
        new Map<ID, Opportunity>();

for(ID opid: OpportunityIDsWithStagenameChanges)
{
    if(!primaryfound.contains(opid))
    {
        if(anyfound.contains(opid))
            OpsWithNoPrimary.put(opid, newmap.get(opid));
        else OpsWithNoContactRoles.put(opid, newmap.get(opid));
    }
}
```

Here we load two new maps based on the primaryfound and anyfound sets. Astute programmers may recognize that there is another way we could do this. Instead of creating two new maps, we could remove entries from clones of the OpportunityIDsWith-StagenameChanges set, and from then on use the newmap variable to obtain records as needed thus eliminating this loop completely. You can see an implementation of that approach in the AfterUpdateOpportunitySets method in the sample code. This potentially leads to a savings of about 200 script lines and the memory consumption of a couple of maps. Enough to be worth doing if you think of it ahead of time, but probably not enough to justify any refactoring later.

Next comes the code to deal with opportunities without contact roles. We first query for any existing tasks on those opportunities, filtering as much as possible to ensure that we only receive the correct type of tasks.

```
// First deal with any opportunities without contact roles
if(OpsWithNoContactRoles.size()>0)
{
```

```
// Find out which ones have existing tasks
List<Task> tasks = [SELECT ID, OwnerID, WhatID,
Status, Subject, Type from Task where Type='Other'
And WhatID in :OpsWithNoContactRoles.keyset() And
IsClosed = False And Subject = 'Assign Primary Contact' ];

// Don't loop through opportunities – waste of
// script lines. Loop through tasks to build set
// of IDs with tasks
Set<ID> opswithtasks = new Set<ID>();
for(Task t: tasks)
{
    Opportunity op = OpsWithNoContactRoles.get(t.WhatID);
    if(t.OwnerID == op.OwnerID) opswithtasks.add(op.ID);
        // Make sure it's assigned to the right person
}
// Now create new tasks
List<Task> newtasks = new List<Task>();
for(Opportunity op: OpsWithNoContactRoles.values())
{
    if(!opswithtasks.contains(op.id))
    {
        newtasks.add(new Task(OwnerID = op.OwnerID,
        Type='Other', WhatID = op.ID, Subject =
        'Assign Primary Contact', ActivityDate =
        Date.Today().AddDays(3) ));
    }
}
if(newtasks.size()>0) insert newtasks;

}
```

One question that you'll often face is choosing which object to loop through. In this case, we're checking each opportunity to see if it has a task. Logically, you might want to loop through each opportunity, and for each opportunity scan the task list to see if a task was found. This approach is fine in a single object scenario, but inefficient in a bulk pattern. In a worst case, where all of the opportunities have existing tasks, the inside of the loop could execute about 200x 100 = 20,000 times (if you have close to 200 tasks in the list, the average number of iterations to find one in a simple search will be about 100). Instead, loop through the tasks and add an entry to the opswithtasks set to determine which opportunities already have a task. The inside of this loop executes a maximum of 200 times.

Only then, do we scan through the opportunities, and create the tasks for those opportunities that do not already have tasks.

The code includes a test to make sure that the task belongs to the owner of the opportunity. Why didn't we include an OwnerID filter in the query? Since we're querying on tasks for multiple opportunities, the filter would have little value. Sure, we could build a set of owners for all of the opportunities we are interested in and filter on that, but we'd still have to do this test in code for each specific opportunity – so there's little benefit.

Be sure to check out the AfterUpdateOpportunitySets method in the sample code for an example of how the logic can be reversed to shave off a few extra lines of code.

Here's a question for you: which implementation of this algorithm is actually better: the AfterUpdateOpportunityCommon method or the AfterUpdateOpportunitySets method? Obviously, AfterUpdateOpportunitySets uses less memory and saves some script lines. But it's also somewhat less intuitive and harder to understand – especially for beginners. Which means the long-term costs to support and maintain the code might be slightly higher.

It's important to not just trade-off limits against each other – you need to also trade them off against the overall lifecycle costs of the software.

Back to the implementation.

First, build a list of the contacts for the opportunities that have no primary contact.

```
if(OpsWithNoPrimary.size()>0)
{
    // Get a list of the contacts
    List<ID> contactidsforops = new List<ID>();
    for(OpportunityContactRole ocr: ocrs)
    {
        if(OpsWithNoPrimary.containskey(ocr.OpportunityID))
                contactidsforops.add(ocr.ContactID);
    }
```

Looping through all of the OpportunityContactRole objects and testing each one against the OpsWithNoPrimary map is potentially inefficient. But to avoid this inefficiency we'd have to either create a map of lists (map of opportunity ID to list of OpportunityContactRole), or requery the Opportunities using a subquery to grab the contact roles. The former would cost more script lines than we would save. The latter would add a query and record lines. So though this code looks inefficient, it's actually a good solution.

In this case, we query on contacts, using a subquery to obtain all of the existing OpportunityContactRole objects for the contact. Note that this will requery OpportunityContactRole objects that we already have – an inefficiency to remember for the next attempt (trading off number of records queried against script lines).

```
// Now query the contacts with their OpportunityContactRoles
    Map<ID, Contact> contactsforops =
        new Map<ID, Contact>([Select ID, (Select ID,
        IsPrimary, OpportunityID from OpportunityContactRoles)
        from Contact where ID in :contactidsforops]);
```

Ultimately, we need to find the best OpportunityContactRole for each opportunity. As with the task example earlier, we need to choose the object for the loop. While you could test each opportunity for its OpportunityContactRoles, it's much more efficient to iterate over OpportunityContactRole and store the ranking of each one in maps that are indexed by Opportunity.

```
// Now figure out which of the
// OpportunityContactRoles should be set
// to primary
Map<ID,OpportunityContactRole> bestocrs =
    new Map<ID, OpportunityContactRole>();
Map<ID,Integer> bestcontactallocrcount =
    new Map<ID,Integer>();
Map<ID,Integer> bestcontactprimaryocrcount =
    new Map<ID, Integer>();
```

```
for(OpportunityContactRole ocr: ocrs)
    {
        if(!OpsWithNoPrimary.containskey(ocr.OpportunityID))
            continue;

        Contact currentcontact =
            contactsforops.get(ocr.ContactID);
        Integer primarycount = 0;
        for(OpportunityContactRole testocr:
                currentcontact.OpportunityContactRoles)
        {
            if(testocr.IsPrimary) primarycount ++;
        }
        if(!bestocrs.containskey(ocr.OpportunityID) ||
            primarycount >
            bestcontactprimaryocrcount.get(ocr.OpportunityID)
            ||
```

```
          (primarycount == bestcontactallocrcount.get(
                  ocr.OpportunityID) &&
          currentcontact.OpportunityContactRoles. size()>
              bestcontactallocrcount.get(ocr.OpportunityID)))
          {
          bestocrs.put(ocr.OpportunityID, ocr);
          bestcontactallocrcount.put(ocr.OpportunityID,
              currentcontact.OpportunityContactRoles.size());
          bestcontactprimaryocrcount.put(
              ocr.OpportunityID, primarycount);
          }
    }
```

There's a small inner loop where we count the primary OpportunityContactRoles for each contact. The total number of OpportunityContactRole objects can be determined by the size of the OpportunityContactRoles array (from the subquery).

Once we've completed the loop, the bestocrs map contains the best OpportunityContactRole for each opportunity. Set it to primary and update them all in one DML operation.

```
    for(OpportunityContactRole best: bestocrs.values())
        best.IsPrimary = true;
    update bestocrs.values();
}
```

The techniques you've seen in this example (and the AfterUpdateOpportunitySets method in the sample code), demonstrate the kinds of design patterns that you will typically see from an experienced Apex developer.

However, in this case, as we've defined the problem and worst case scenario, common bulk design patterns simply aren't good enough.

Experimenting with the test code demonstrates that this solution is fine in terms of number of SOQL calls. The number of script lines (and associated CPU time) is still high and the number of SOQL rows retrieved is still a concern, but it's not clear yet how big a problem each one will be.

Query Optimization

Usually when you see issues with CPU time, the problem is usually either a nested loop, or a loop over a very large number of objects. In this case, we have a bit of both.

Ignore the first part of the code where the requirement for dealing with opportunities without contact roles is addressed – that code is not causing the problem.

In the second part that deals with opportunities without primary contacts, the outer loop iterates over OpportunityContactRole objects. In this scenario, with up to 200 opportunities with 20 contact roles each, that's a 4000 object loop. If you're targeting a maximum of 1 second of CPU time, that's 250 microseconds per object per iteration. That doesn't leave a lot of extra room.

Within this loop, there is another loop, that iterates over the OpportunityContactRole objects for a single contact to count the number of times it is the primary contact. In our scenario that can be 100 objects. So, even though it is a very tight loop, it alone is a major contributor to the CPU time used.

Can this be improved?

The AfterUpdateOpportunityBetterQueries demonstrates how to address both SOQL rows and CPU time issues.

First, you can get rid of the inner loop by using SOQL aggregate functions. The count function allows you to count the number of records that match the specified filter, in this case: IsPrimary = true.

But SOQL aggregate functions can't be placed in a subquery. So to use this approach, the algorithm has to be redesigned. You still need to be able to obtain the count based on the contact, so after doing the query, you'll need to copy the totals into maps that are indexed by the contact ID.

```
List<AggregateResult> ocrsbycontact = [Select ContactID,
    Count(ID) total from OpportunityContactRole where
    ContactID in :contactidsforops Group By ContactID];

List<AggregateResult> primaryocrsbycontact =
    [Select ContactID, Count(ID) total from
    OpportunityContactRole where IsPrimary=true and
    ContactID in :contactidsforops
    Group By ContactID];

// Let's get the totals by contact for faster loop
Map<ID, Integer> totalsbycontact = new Map<ID, Integer>();
Map<ID, Integer> primarybycontact = new Map<ID, Integer>();

for(AggregateResult ar: ocrsbycontact)
    totalsbycontact.put((ID)ar.get('ContactID'),
    Integer.ValueOf(ar.get('total')));

for(AggregateResult ar: primaryocrsbycontact)
    primarybycontact.put((ID)ar.get('ContactID'),
    Integer.ValueOf(ar.get('total')));
```

What are the tradeoffs in this approach? There are two extra queries, but that only brings the total number of queries to four, so
that's insignificant. There are two new loops that together iterate
over twice the total number of contacts. In our worst case scenario,
that is 200 opportunities x 20 contact roles each. Even if each
contact role is a distinct contact, that is 4000 rows. Both are not
only very tight loops, they are performing map inserts, which are
very efficient operations. At 10000 script lines you might be looking at 20 milliseconds or so. This replaces a possible 4000 object x
100 iteration loop = 400,000 script lines or about 800 milliseconds. An excellent trade.

What about the rest of the algorithm? Can we reduce the number
of objects that are being iterated?

Yes and no.

You still need to check all 4000 possible OpportunityContactRole
objects to see which is most efficient. But you can potentially reduce the amount of code within the loop further.

Previously, the sample looped over all OpportunityContactRoles,
and did a test within the loop to determine whether to continue or
not:

```
if(!OpsWithNoPrimary.containskey(ocr.OpportunityID))
    continue;
```

You can get rid of that line by using the Set approach and modifying the set to contain opportunities without primary contacts, but
that do have some contacts.

```
for(OpportunityContactRole ocr: ocrs)
{
    if(ocr.IsPrimary)
```

```
        OpsWithNoPrimaryWithContactRoles.remove(
        ocr.OpportunityID);

    OpsWithNoContactRoles.remove(ocr.OpportunityID);
}


OpsWithNoPrimaryWithContactRoles.RemoveAll(
    OpsWithNoContactRoles);
```

Now that you have maps to look up the totals for contacts, you don't need a subquery on the OpportunityContactRole query. What you actually need is a way to obtain a list of OpportunityContactRole objects for each opportunity. You can change the query to opportunities with a subquery on OpportunityContactRole.

```
for(Opportunity op: OpportunitiesWithoutPrimary)
{
    OpportunityContactRole bestocr = null;
    Integer primarycount = 0;
    Integer totalcount = 0;
    for(OpportunityContactRole opocrs:
            op.OpportunityContactRoles)
    {
        if(bestocr==null ||
        primarybycontact.get(opocrs.contactid) > primarycount ||
        (primarybycontact.get(opocrs.contactid) == totalcount &&
        totalsbycontact.get(opocrs.contactid) > totalcount ))
            primarycount = primarybycontact.get(opocrs.contactid);
            totalcount = totalsbycontact.get(opocrs.contactid);
            bestocr = opocrs;
    }
    bestocr.IsPrimary = true;
    ocrstoupdate.add(bestocr);
}
update ocrstoupdate;
```

In terms of the code itself, there will be little savings in the worst case scenario where every opportunity needs to have a primary contact role assigned. However, in any case where only some of the opportunities need primary contact roles assigned, you'll definitely see a performance boost.

It may seem odd to do an Opportunity query just to essentially map from opportunities to OpportunityContactRole objects. After all, you already have the opportunities (it is an opportunity trigger), and you've already queried for the OpportunityContactRole objects. Why not create a map where the key is the opportunity ID and the values are lists of OpportunityContactRole objects?

```
Map<ID,List<OpportunityContactRole>>
```

This is another limits tradeoff. Building a map would save a SOQL query and reduce the number of query rows retrieved, but at the cost of additional CPU time. Both are good approaches.

Into the Future

The current implementation is already fairly solid. But you won't always be able to reduce CPU time through the use of SOQL aggregation. Here's another approach you can use.

One of the advantages of future (asynchronous) calls is that they have higher limits. In this particular case, there is no reason why the operation has to take place immediately. So why not move it into a future call?

Refactoring this code into a future call is remarkably easy.

The start of the function is changed as follows:

```
public static void
    AfterUpdateOpportunityFutureSupport(
    List<Opportunity> newlist, Map<ID, Opportunity> newmap,
    Map<ID, Opportunity> oldmap)
{
    // Pattern 4 — with future support

    Set<ID> OpportunityIDsWithStagenameChanges = new Set<ID>();

    // Get OpportunityContactRoles
    if(!System.isFuture())
    {
        for(Opportunity op: newlist)
        {
            if(op.StageName != oldmap.get(op.id).StageName)
                OpportunityIDsWithStagenameChanges.add(op.id);
        }
        if(newlist.size()>100)
        {
            if(!FutureCalled)
                FutureUpdateOpportunities(
                OpportunityIDsWithStagenameChanges);
            FutureCalled = true;
            return;
        }
    }
    else OpportunityIDsWithStagenameChanges.addall(
            newmap.keyset());
```

This implementation starts by detecting whether or not it is a future call. If not, it looks for the stage changes to obtain a list of effected opportunities (as before). In this example, there's a fixed threshold to determine whether to go with a future call or not – I'll come back to that shortly.

If a future call is needed, the set of opportunity IDs are passed as arguments to the future call, and the function exits. There's a static variable test to make sure the future call happens only once – just in case this trigger is reentered due to a DML update by another trigger, or a field update in a workflow.

If this is a future call, the OpportunityIDsWithStagenameChanges variable is loaded with the IDs of the opportunities to process and the function continues as before.

The asynchronous function is quite simple:

```
@future
public static void FutureUpdateOpportunities(
    Set<ID> opportunitiyids)
{
    Map<ID, Opportunity> newmap = new Map<ID,Opportunity>(
    [SELECT ID, OwnerID from Opportunity
        where ID in :opportunitiyids]);

    AfterUpdateOpportunityFutureSupport(
        newmap.values(), newmap, null);
}
private static Boolean FutureCalled = false;
```

Remember to include any opportunity fields used within the AfterUpdateOpportunityFutureSupport function in the Select query.

In this example, we used a fixed threshold to determine whether to perform a future call or not, but you have many other options. You can use a custom setting to make this number configurable. You can use a Limits function to determine dynamically whether you are approaching limits as the code runs. If you see that you are getting close, you can abort the operation and make the future call instead.

You don't have to make it an all or nothing decision. You could process the opportunities without contact roles (creating tasks as necessary) within the trigger, and only process those without primary contacts in the future call. This would be a great approach if, instead of creating tasks, you wanted to mark those records as errors (something that must be done immediately).

You could add some other optimizations at this point. For example, the FutureUpdateOpportunities function could include a subquery on OpportunityContactRoles, thus allowing you to eliminate an extra query later.

The ability to quickly refactor code is yet another reason why all of your trigger functionality should be implemented in class methods.

Batch Apex

Future calls are a great way to handle CPU time limits, but in this example, we're also concerned about the limit to the number of records that can be retrieved in an execution context. Unfortunately, this limit is a tough one to test for – the number of records that you can insert using your test code is less than the limit on the number you can retrieve. So the only ways to detect potential record limit issues are by evaluating worst case scenarios (as we did earlier), or by running the tests on existing data in a large organization that happens to generate that worst case scenario.

The way to handle processing of large numbers of records is to split them up into smaller batches using Batch Apex.

The trigger processing code uses almost exactly the same design pattern as the future call did, as shown in the AfterUpdateOpportunityBatchSupport method:

```
private static Boolean BatchCalled = false;

public static void AfterUpdateOpportunityBatchSupport(
    List<Opportunity> newlist, Map<ID, Opportunity>
    newmap, Map<ID, Opportunity> oldmap)
    {
    // Pattern 6 - with batch support

    Set<ID> OpportunityIDsWithStagenameChanges = new Set<ID>();

    // Get OpportunityContactRoles
    if(!System.isBatch())
    {
        for(Opportunity op: newlist)
        {
            if(op.StageName != oldmap.get(op.id).StageName)
                OpportunityIDsWithStagenameChanges.add(op.id);
        }
        if(newlist.size()>100)
        {
            if(!BatchCalled)
            {
                Database.executeBatch(new BulkPatternBatch(
                    OpportunityIDsWithStagenameChanges), 100);
            }
            BatchCalled = true;
            return;
        }
    }
    else
        OpportunityIDsWithStagenameChanges.addall(
            newmap.keyset());
```

The second parameter in the Database.executeBatch call specifies the size of the batch to use. Choose a small enough size to ensure that you won't exceed the record count limit.

The batch class itself is fairly simple. The query and set of opportunity IDs are initialized by the class constructor and are stored in the class. The execute method is called with a subset of records based on the batch size. It then calls the AfterUpdateOpportunityBatchSupport method.

```
global class BulkPatternBatch implements
   Database.Batchable<sObject> {

   global final string query;
   global final Set<ID> opportunityids;

   public BulkPatternBatch(Set<ID> opportunityIDsToUpdate)
   {
      opportunityids = opportunityIDsToUpdate;
      query = 'SELECT ID, OwnerID from Opportunity
               where ID in :opportunityids ';
   }

   global Database.QueryLocator start(
               Database.BatchableContext BC){
      return Database.getQueryLocator(query);
   }

   global void execute(Database.BatchableContext BC,
                     List<sObject> scope){
      List<Opportunity> ops = (List<Opportunity>)scope;
      Map<ID, Opportunity> newmap =
         new Map<ID, Opportunity>(ops);
      ThinkingInApexBulkPatterns.
      AfterUpdateOpportunityBatchSupport(ops, newmap, null);
      return;
   }

   global void finish(Database.BatchableContext BC){
```

```
    }
}
```

Keep in mind that test code can only execute a single batch iteration. So be sure that your test code batch size does not exceed the batch size specified in the Database.executeBatch method.

Other Approaches

What if you absolutely can't find a way to solve a limits issue? As you have seen, it is important to design your code based on worst –case bulk scenarios. But those worst-case scenarios have to be realistic. The very fact that there are limits means that you can rarely code against theoretical worst-case scenarios.

If you are a consultant developing code for a single organization, your job is relatively easy. You can run some reports against the actual organization. In this example, you would probably find that while one or two opportunities have twenty contacts, the average is actually two or three. And that the average number of opportunities for a given contact is also two or three. On finding that, you might generously allow for six of each and stop with the initial simple scenario (though not the awful one!)

But if you are writing software for a package to use on multiple organizations, your challenge is much greater – as you have to anticipate the realistic worst-case scenario for any organization.

What if even these approaches won't work? There are still other options to try.

- You can store intermediate information in custom objects. Then use scheduled Apex to query for those objects, executing the required operations in smaller batches than are even possible using Batch Apex. It might take a while though – as the number of scheduled operations is also limited.

- You can use an external service. A future call can make a callout into an external web-service. You can host external functionality there to perform complex tasks either immediately, or in the background. After completion of the background operations, your external service can use the API to update data within the Salesforce instance.

- If you are building a package, you can implement multiple solutions and choose the right one for a particular organization after deployment using your package configuration.

- You can build a standalone utility program that performs operations either using the API, or on data exported using the Apex dataloader.

Don't expect to come up with the perfect solution the first time around. It is very common for even the most advanced developers to assess multiple designs, and to even prototype and implement several different approaches in order to come up with the best solution for a particular problem. Adopting bulk patterns and considering limits from the start doesn't mean your first attempt will be your final implementation, only that your path to a good solution will be faster and your final implementation more likely to work well.

Bulk Patterns and Web Services

Apex allows you to expose methods as global web services using both SOAP and REST. Most of the examples illustrate how to do so using single object or single value parameters. Don't follow those examples.

In addition to the limits I have already discussed, web service calls on most organizations are subject to 24 hour limits to the number of calls that can be processed. They are also subject to limits on the amount of data that can be transferred by a single call. These two limits help define the way you should design web service calls.

First, as with triggers, all web service calls should be designed for bulk processing. Both SOAP and REST web services support lists of primitive and SObject types as both parameters and return types. You web service interface will be more efficient, easier to develop and support, and more scalable if you avoid single object patterns entirely and only build bulk web service calls.

At the same time, you should specify the maximum number of items in your parameter lists to ensure that you don't exceed other limits. In particular, be sure to keep an eye on CPU time limits – many of the functions used to support web services, such as serialization and encryption, are particularly CPU intensive. You should validate the length of input lists to make sure those limits aren't exceeded, and return or throw errors if necessary.

Part II – Application Architecture and Patterns

In Part I of this book, you learned to think in Apex. This means that when faced with a software challenge, you know that your solution must be built to fit within the constraints of one or more execution contexts, each of which has a set of limits. You know that, with rare exceptions, your design will have to handle large numbers of objects. You know that static variables in Apex work differently from other languages, and that difference is a critical and essential part of Apex programming.

These are the core, fundamental concepts that every Apex programmer has to not just know, but understand so deeply it becomes second nature.

Now that you can think in Apex, it's time to look at how one builds solutions in Apex. To do so, we will look at both architecture and common design patterns.

At first, I considered separating those into two parts of the book – chapters on architecture that focused on the higher level structure of Apex applications, and chapters that discussed common software patterns. But after some thought, I decided to combine the two, mixing the discussion of high level design patterns with the code patterns used to implement them. I believe that viewing these together will help clarify the thought processes one can bring to Apex design.

This part of the book is also not a comprehensive treatment of every possible Apex design pattern. The number of subsystems left out, VisualForce, Email, Chatter, and so on, probably exceed those that are included. However, as discussed in the introduction, the goal here is not to replace the Salesforce documentation, but rather to focus on, and elaborate on, the core language features. I think you'll find that your understanding of the design issues discussed in this part of the book will translate nicely to those other subsystems, and make them easier to learn and use effectively.

5 – Fun With Collections

You've already seen quite a few bulk patterns. The one thing they all have in common is extensive use of collections.

The Apex collection types: maps, sets and lists, all have their little quirks. Here are some of the issues that you may run into.

Using Maps to Obtain Sets

One of the most common operations in Apex involves retrieving a related list of objects. In this example, assume you have a list of contacts and wish to retrieve the related tasks. You certainly wouldn't use a loop to perform a query for each contact, as that would quickly fail in a bulk operation. Instead, you need a list or set of the contact IDs, so that you can retrieve all of the tasks for those contacts in one query. You could build the set and perform the query like this:

```
Set<ID> contactids = new Set<ID>();
for(Contact ct: cts) contactids.add(ct.id);

List<Task> tasks = [Select ID from Task where Whoid
                    in :contactids Limit 500];
```

But in most cases you'll prefer to do it like this:

```
Map<ID, Contact> contactmap = new Map<ID,
        Contact>(cts);

List<Task> tasks2 = [Select ID from Task
      where Whoid in :contactmap.keyset() Limit 500];
```

When you pass a list as a constructor parameter to a newly created map with an ID key, the map is created using the ID property of the object as the map key. Using a map in this manner is a slightly inefficient use of memory (assuming you don't actually need the map itself), but it does save quite a few script lines as it avoids the need of a loop to populate a set.

Grouping Objects

You've already seen how you can use SOQL to efficiently group related objects. There are some cases, however, where you will find yourself needing to group objects using Apex code.

One example is where your algorithm requires you have all of the objects in a single array. In that case, you have a choice: use a Group By SOQL query and then loop through and build a single list of all the related objects, or do a SOQL query without the Group By term, and do your own grouping.

In some cases, you may need records with different groupings, and you may find it more efficient to do your own grouping than to perform multiple SOQL queries.

Finally, you may want to group on a term that isn't supported in SOQL at all. For example, let's say you want to look at all of the tasks for a group of contacts. These contacts may be specified in a trigger, a batch call, an external API call or even a VisualForce page. First, you want to perform a global operation on the tasks, where you don't care about the source. Next, you want to perform an operation on them grouped by the week in which they occur (displaying them in a VisualForce calendar, for example).

The solution is to create a map, where the key is the start date of the week and the value is a list of tasks.

```
// cts is the list of input contacts
Map<ID, Contact> contactmap = new Map<ID, Contact>(cts);

List<Task> tasks = [Select ID, ActivityDate,
            Description from Task where
            Whoid in :contactmap.keyset()
            Order By ActivityDate
            Desc Limit 500];

Map<Date, List<Task>> tasksbyweek = new Map<Date, List<Task>>();

for(Task t: tasks)
{
    // Perform global task operation here

    // Group by week
    Date weekstart = t.ActivityDate.toStartOfWeek();
    if(tasksbyweek.get(weekstart)==null)
        tasksbyweek.put(weekstart, new List<Task>());
    tasksbyweek.get(weekstart).add(t);

    // Perform week related operation here
}
```

Ordering the original list of tasks by ActivityDate results in each of the weekly task lists being in order as well.

This approach results in a sparse list of weeks. In other words – weeks for which there is no task do not have entries in the tasksbyweek map. In a calendar application, you could take a slightly different approach: initially creating entries for each week in the year, and filtering the task query to allow only tasks within that year. This would eliminate the need for testing the presence of a key/list while doing the grouping, which can lead to a slight efficiency improvement when processing large number of tasks.

Case Sensitivity

Keys on maps are case sensitive, except when they are not.

Generally speaking, the keys on a map are case sensitive. Thus the following test code succeeds:

```
static testMethod void casesensitivity()
{
    Map<String,Integer> intmap =
        new Map<String,Integer>{'A'=>0, 'b'=>1,'C'=>2};
    system.assert(!intmap.containskey('a'));
    system.assert(!intmap.containskey('B'));
}
```

B is not b. A is not a.

However, there are some specific cases where a map is case insensitive. For example, when using dynamic Apex to obtain describe information.

```
static testMethod void caseOnDescribe() {
    // Get global describe
    Map<String, Schema.SObjectType>
        gd = Schema.getGlobalDescribe();
    System.Assert(gd.ContainsKey('CampaignMember'));
    System.Assert(gd.ContainsKey('campaignmember'));
    System.Assert(gd.ContainsKey('CAMPAIGNMEMBER'));
```

These asserts all pass, indicating that the lookup is case insensitive. This also applies when using the getMap method on an SObject type.

Internally, the object names are stored in lower case, something you can easily verify by adding the statement system.debug(gd); and looking at the debug output for the map. This an interesting side effect if you use the following code:

```
System.Assert(gd.keyset().Contains('campaignmember'));
System.Assert(!gd.keyset().Contains('CampaignMember'));
System.Assert(!gd.keyset().Contains('CAMPAIGNMEMBER'));
}
```

Though logically the statements gd.ContainsKey and gd.keyset().contains are equivalent, in this case the latter is case sensitive and the former is not.

These are issues to keep in mind when using dynamic SOQL – which is particularly common when creating packages.

As an aside, keep in mind that effective API 28 (Summer 13), the keys for the map returned by the getGlobalDescribe function always contain the namespace of the object if it is part of a managed package.

Avoid Using Objects as Keys

Apex allows you to use objects as map keys and to store objects in sets. But don't do it. Here's why.

Let's say you have a list of contacts, and you need to store an integer value for each object using a map. Your code might look something like this:

```
static testMethod void objectKeys()
    {
        List<Contact>cts = new List<Contact>();
        for(Integer x=0;x<5;x++)
        {
            cts.add(new Contact(LastName = 'cttest_' +
                    String.valueOf(x)));
```

```
    }
 insert cts;

// Create a map keyed on contacts
Map<Contact, Integer> contactmap =
        new Map<Contact, Integer>();

for(Integer x = 0; x< 5; x++)
{
    contactmap.put(cts[x], x);
}

system.assertEquals(contactmap.size(),5);
```

So far, so good. But let's say you modify the object, either directly or through a reference from a different variable. In this case, the samecontacts array contains references to the same objects. You then modify one of the fields on the object (either through the original reference or through the new one – it doesn't matter).

```
// Create another list to reference these
   List<Contact> samecontacts = new List<Contact>(cts);

   for(Integer x = 0; x< 5; x++)
   {
       samecontacts[x].AssistantName =
           'person' + string.ValueOf(x);
```

First, assert that the change applied to the object itself regardless of which array you use to reference it. Since we made a copy (not a clone), this works correctly.

```
       system.assertEquals(cts[x].AssistantName,
           samecontacts[x].AssistantName);
```

Now use the object to look up its value in the contactmap. The value should be there and should retrieve the integer value, but it doesn't. In fact, the lookup returns null.

```
system.assertNotEquals(contactmap.get(cts[x]), x);
```

Go ahead and add the revised object into the map.

```
contactmap.put(samecontacts[x], x);
}
```

As this assert shows, entering the modified object caused a new entry to exist in the map. The contactmap size is now 10.

```
system.assertNotEquals(contactmap.size(),5);
}
```

You can see this same phenomena with sets as well in the FunWithCollections.objectSets example in the sample code.

Apex uses a hash of the field values as the internal value to use when searching for the object in the map or set. Changing a field on an object changes this hash value, causing the same object to appear as two distinct objects when used as keys.

Given that one of the main purposes of maps and sets when used with objects is to hold them while they are being modified, using objects as keys or in sets is a sure way to create subtle and hard to find bugs.

The right design pattern is to use the object ID as the key or set value. A correct implementation of the ObjectKeys class is shown here:

```
static testMethod void objectKeysCorrect()
{
    List<Contact>cts = new List<Contact>();
    for(Integer x=0;x<5;x++)
    {
        cts.add(new Contact(LastName = 'cttest_' +
                String.valueOf(x)));
    }

    insert cts;

    // Create a map keyed on contacts
    Map<ID, Integer> contactmap = new Map<ID, Integer>();

    for(Integer x = 0; x< 5; x++)
    {
        contactmap.put(cts[x].id, x);
    }

    system.assertEquals(contactmap.size(),5);

    // Create another list to reference these
    List<Contact> samecontacts = new List<Contact>(cts);

    for(Integer x = 0; x< 5; x++)
    {
        samecontacts[x].AssistantName = 'person' +
        string.ValueOf(x);
        system.assertEquals(cts[x].AssistantName,
            samecontacts[x].AssistantName);
        system.assertEquals(contactmap.get(cts[x].id), x);
        contactmap.put(samecontacts[x].id, x);
    }
    system.assertEquals(contactmap.size(),5);
}
```

As you can see, the lookup within the final loop now works (assertEquals instead of assertNotEquals), and the final number of entries in the map is 5.

This presents an interesting dilemma when dealing with objects that you have not yet inserted (and thus have no ID). If the object has a unique field, such as account number, you may be able to use that field as a key. Otherwise, your best bet is to leave the objects in a list and reference them by location. In this example, where you want to associate an integer with each contact, use the position of the contact as the map key in a Map<Integer,Integer> map.

Keeping Track of Objects to Update

It's very common to update objects in triggers and other Apex code. It's always a good idea to only update those objects that are actually changed. That improves the efficiency and performance of your code, and reduces the number of DML records touched, helping you stay within limits.

Logically, the way to do this is simple: any time you update a field in an object, place that object in a collection of objects that need updating. Then, at the end of the Apex Code, update them all in a single DML operation.

For a simple trigger case, a list of objects to update might seem the best way to go.

```
List<Contact>contactstoupdate = new List<Contact>();

for(Contact ct: cts)
{
    // Do various operations
    // If an update is needed:
    contactstoupdate.add(ct);
```

```
}
```

```
if(contactstoupdate.size()>0) update contactstoupdate;
```

But as you'll see in the next chapter, there are good reasons to design your code so that you can add functionality to a trigger, or combine all of the updates required by several distinct triggers or classes into a single update operation. For this reason, you should always use a map that is keyed to the object ID (or other unique field).

```
Map<ID,Contact> contactstoupdate = new Map<ID, Contact>();

// First set of operations
for(Contact ct: cts)
{
    // Do various operations
    // If an update is needed:
    contactstoupdate.put(ct.id, ct);

}

// Second set of operations
for(Contact ct: cts)
{
    // Do various operations
    // If an update is needed:
    contactstoupdate.put(ct.id, ct);

}

if(contactstoupdate.size()>0)
    update contactstoupdate.values();
```

You can't use a list, because you can't have the same object twice in a list during a DML operation. You can't use a set because, as you saw in the previous section, field modifications can cause two identical objects to be seen as unique, leading again to duplicate objects in the set.

6 – Triggers

It's a rare application that doesn't involve the creation of one or more triggers. There are other ways for Apex code to run in a system, but none of them are more important to do correctly. If you have an exception in a VisualForce controller, you may see an error message on a page. If you have an exception in a webservice class, calls to that class may fail. But if you have an exception in a trigger, your organization's users may no longer be able to perform even simple operations using the standard Salesforce user interface.

One Trigger to Rule Them All

The first and most important thing to know about triggers is that when you have more than one trigger of the same type, you cannot predict the order in which they will fire.

In a perfect world, this would not matter. Each trigger's code would be completely independent of the others and there would be no possibility that they could interfere with each other. In a perfect world, external factors, such as workflows or triggers written by other developers, couldn't interfere with the operation of your code.

But this is not a perfect world. You can't control the order in which triggers are fired. This can be a very serious problem. What if there is an order dependency with the triggers you've built? You may never know it, because you can't write test code that specifies the order in which your triggers are fired. If there is a problem, it might not appear until you've deployed the code into production. And even then, it may present itself as an intermittent error that is virtually impossible to catch in a debug log and is impossible to reproduce.

You also can't prevent other system administrators from creating triggers and workflows. If you are creating a package, you have no control over what exists on the target system. Learning to deal with these possibilities (as much as is possible) will be an ongoing theme throughout the rest of this book.

While you can't achieve perfect control over an organization, you can, at least, take control over your own code.

Figure 6-1 illustrates the non-deterministic nature of triggers, where the order in which they execute cannot be predicted.

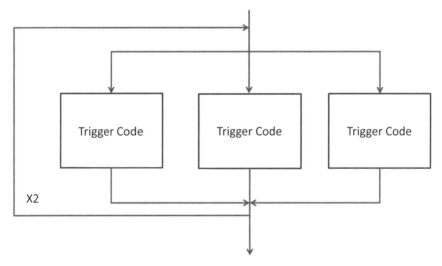

Figure 6-1 –The order in which triggers occur is non-deterministic

In Chapter 2, the discussion of static variables offered one reason to place trigger code into a class. Figure 6-2 illustrates how you can extend that approach to combining the functionality from several triggers into one.

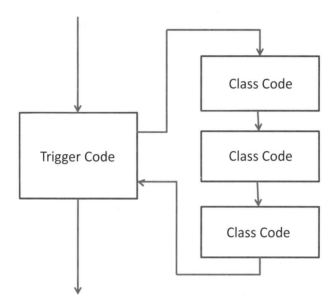

Figure 6-2 –The preferred design pattern for triggers

This approach guarantees you predictability within your application. But it has other benefits as well.

Let's say that this is an update trigger where each functional block may perform an update on a related object. If each functional block is in its own trigger, you can end up with three DML updates. Aside from drawing against your available limits, each of those updates will potentially spawn off additional workflows and trigger executions.

Figure 6-3 illustrates a better approach. You can define a collection to hold all of the objects to be updated. The collection can be a static class variable or you can pass it as a parameter to each of the class methods.

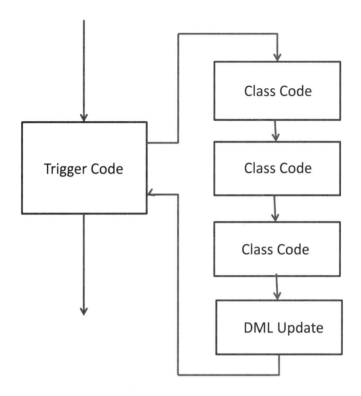

Figure 6-3 –One DML update can be shared among functional blocks

Once all of the classes have completed their operations, a single DML update handles all of the updates at once.

Let's look at some approaches you can use to implement this design.

Architecture and Triggers

There are a number of viable architectures for implementing tightly controlled execution flow within a trigger.

Let's say you have two operations to perform during an after-update trigger on an opportunity. Either of these operations might need to perform an additional update on the opportunity or a related object (such as the account or primary contact). The code should be designed so that it is easy to add additional functionality to the trigger later - anywhere in the sequence of operations.

You could implement this functionality as follows:

In the trigger

```
Map<ID, Opportunity> objectstoupdate =
    new Map<ID, Opportunity>();
TriggerArchitectureClass1.Entry1(trigger.new, trigger.newmap,
    trigger.old, trigger.oldmap, objectstoupdate);
TriggerArchitectureClass2.Entry1(trigger.new, trigger.newmap,
    trigger.old, trigger.oldmap, objectstoupdate);
if(objectstoupdate.size()>0) update objectstoupdate.values();
```

Where each operation is implemented in a class that follows this pattern:

```
public class TriggerArchitectureClass1 {

    public static void Entry1(
        List<Opportunity> newlist, Map<ID, Opportunity> newmap,
        List<Opportunity> oldlist, Map<ID,Opportunity> oldmap,
        Map<ID, Opportunity> objectstoupdate)
    {
        // Do some processing here
        // Add entries to the objectstoupdate map
        //if they need to be updated
    }
}
```

This approach isn't terrible. It does allow you to control the flow of execution and makes it easy to change the order or add or remove functionality. It does aggregate DML operations.

The approach does have a weakness. It is limited to aggregating updates to one type of object. What if one or more of the classes needs to update a related object such as the opportunity account? You would have to add another parameter to each of the class entry methods. This approach also violates the principle of reducing the amount of code in triggers.

A better approach is to use another class to act as a dispatcher for triggers. Your trigger code will now look like this:

```
TriggerArchitectureMain1.Entry2(trigger.new,
    trigger.newmap, trigger.old, trigger.oldmap);
```

The dispatcher code would look something like this:

```
public class TriggerArchitectureMain1 {
    public static Map<ID, Opportunity>
        opstoupdate = new Map<ID, Opportunity>();

    public static void Entry2(List<Opportunity>
        newlist, Map<ID, Opportunity> newmap,
        List<Opportunity> oldlist, Map<ID,Opportunity> oldmap)
    {
        TriggerArchitectureClass1.Entry2(newlist,
            newmap, oldlist, oldmap);
        TriggerArchitectureClass2.Entry2(newlist,
            newmap, oldlist, oldmap);
        if(opstoupdate.size()>0)
            update opstoupdate.values();
    }
}
```

Now each of the functional blocks (represented by the TriggerArchitectureClass*n*.Entry2 methods) can add objects to the opstoupdate map by referencing the TriggerArchitecture-Main1.opstoupdate static variable directly. If you need to keep track of more objects, or share other data between the functional blocks, you can easily add additional static variables.

At first glance, this may seem like a great deal of fuss over a fairly minor issue. But this architecture - using centralized dispatching for trigger functionality, turns out to have profound implications.

Controlling Program Flow

Figure 6-3 illustrated the concept of caching DML updates across functional blocks. This is one good way to control your execution flow, as it eliminates additional trigger calls and workflows during your trigger processing.

However, there are cases where you will want to perform DML updates during trigger execution. One obvious example is where you want changes in the database from one block of code to be reflected in a query during a subsequent block. This scenario is illustrated in Figure 6-4.

The additional triggers and workflows fired by the DML updates will run additional Apex code. They might even reenter the current trigger (which would lead to an infinite loop on other platforms, but will be self-limiting on Force.com).

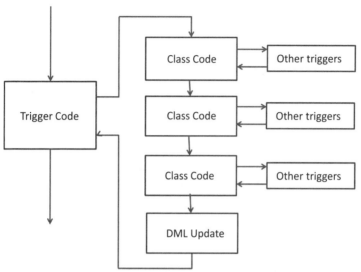

Figure 6-4 – DML operations have side effects

This raises the question: what do you actually want to have happen when your code performs a DML operation? Do you actually want to process those other triggers? Would you prefer to ignore them? One way or another, there's a good chance that you would want some special handling when they occur based on the knowledge that the trigger was raised due to your own DML call.

How can a trigger differentiate between an external event and one caused by your own DML operation? By now the answer should be obvious. Trigger events caused by a DML operation share the same execution context as the DML operation. So the answer is to use a static variable.

There are many ways to implement this kind of special handling. Here's a very simplistic approach that takes advantage of our earlier decision to centralize dispatching of trigger functionality:

```
public static Boolean InClass1 = false;
public static Boolean InClass2 = false;
public static void Entry3(List<Opportunity> newlist,
```

```
   Map<ID, Opportunity> newmap, List<Opportunity>
   oldlist, Map<ID,Opportunity> oldmap)
{
   if(!InClass1)
   {
      InClass1= true;
      TriggerArchitectureClass1.Entry3(newlist,
         newmap, oldlist, oldmap);
      InClass1 = false;
   }
   InClass2 = true;
   TriggerArchitectureClass2.Entry3(newlist, newmap,
      oldlist, oldmap);
   InClass2 = false;
   if(opstoupdate.size()>0)
      update opstoupdate.values();
}
```

This example demonstrates how you could prevent reentrancy into the TriggerArchitecture1 class. It would be just as easy to call a different method on TriggerArchitecture1, or a method on a different class entirely. In this example, reentrancy is still allowed into the TriggerArchitecture2 class, but now that class can examine the InClass2 static variable to determine whether the call is reentrant and act accordingly.

As you see, centralized dispatching of triggers has now taken us beyond just controlling the order of operations within a trigger. It's given us a tool to detect and control the order and operation of subsequent triggers caused by DML operations in our code. More important, it has given us a tool to completely ignore those triggers, which can go a long way towards simplifying testing requirements.

Really Controlling Program Flow

The solution so far is decent, and it goes a long way towards centralizing control over program flow. But in a large application with a variety of triggers on different objects, you can still end up with multiple dispatch functions managing numerous static variables. So you can end up with quite a bit of complexity.

So let's take this approach to its logical conclusion. What if every trigger went through a centralized dispatch function? If no operation is currently in progress, forward the trigger to a series of classes to perform the desired operation. If an operation is currently in progress (i.e. the trigger was caused by a DML operation), call back into the currently executing class and let it decide whether or not to process the trigger.

You can adopt this approach by defining an interface that will be implemented by your various class functions. The interface might look something like this:

```
public interface ITriggerEntry
{
    void MainEntry(String TriggerObject,
        Boolean IsBefore, Boolean IsDelete,
        Boolean IsAfter, Boolean IsInsert,
        Boolean IsUpdate, Boolean IsExecuting,
        List<SObject> newlist, Map<ID, SObject> newmap,
        List<SObject> oldlist, Map<ID,SObject> oldmap);

    void InProgressEntry(String TriggerObject,
        Boolean IsBefore, Boolean IsDelete,
        Boolean IsAfter, Boolean IsInsert,
        Boolean IsUpdate, Boolean IsExecuting,
        List<SObject> newlist, Map<ID, SObject> newmap,
        List<SObject> oldlist, Map<ID,SObject> oldmap);
}
```

You can then build a single trigger for any object and event in which you are interested. The opportunity trigger could look like this:

```
trigger OnOpportunity2 on Opportunity
    (after update, before update, after insert, before insert) {

    TriggerArchitectureMain1.Entry4('Opportunity',
        trigger.IsBefore, trigger.IsDelete,
        trigger.isAfter, trigger.IsInsert,
        trigger.IsUpdate, trigger.IsExecuting,
        trigger.new, trigger.newmap, trigger.old,
        trigger.oldmap);
}
```

The dispatcher function, that is called by every trigger in your application, stores a reference to the currently executing class in the activefunction static variable. If this variable is set when the function is called, you know that this trigger was caused by that function. In this design, the trigger information is forwarded back to the originating function for processing.

```
public static ITriggerEntry activefunction = null;

public static void Entry4(String TriggerObject,
    Boolean IsBefore, Boolean IsDelete,
    Boolean IsAfter, Boolean IsInsert,
    Boolean IsUpdate, Boolean IsExecuting,
    List<SObject> newlist, Map<ID, SObject> newmap,
    List<SObject> oldlist, Map<ID,SObject> oldmap)
{
    if(activefunction != null)
    {
        activefunction.InProgressEntry(TriggerObject,
            IsBefore, IsDelete, IsAfter, IsInsert,
```

```
            IsUpdate, IsExecuting, newlist, newmap,
            oldlist, oldmap);
            return;
    }
```

If this trigger was not a result of your function, it gets dispatched to one or more classes for processing.

```
    if(TriggerObject == 'Opportunity' && IsAfter
            && IsUpdate)
    {
        activefunction = new triggerArchitectureClass1();

        activefunction.MainEntry(TriggerObject,
            IsBefore, IsDelete, IsAfter, IsInsert,
            IsUpdate, IsExecuting,  newlist, newmap,
            oldlist, oldmap);

        activefunction = new TriggerArchitectureClass2();
        activefunction.MainEntry(TriggerObject,
            IsBefore, IsDelete, IsAfter, IsInsert,
            IsUpdate, IsExecuting,  newlist, newmap,
            oldlist, oldmap);
```

Note that you are now creating instances of the classes instead of using static methods. Of course, nothing is to prevent you from continuing to cache results for centralized updating.

```
        if(opstoupdate.size()>0)
            update opstoupdate.values();
        activefunction = null;
    }
}
```

Now let's look at a class implementation.

```
public class TriggerArchitectureClass1 implements
    TriggerArchitectureMain1.ITriggerEntry
{

    public void MainEntry(String TriggerObject,
        Boolean IsBefore, Boolean IsDelete,
        Boolean IsAfter, Boolean IsInsert,
        Boolean IsUpdate, Boolean IsExecuting,
        List<SObject> newlist, Map<ID, SObject> newmap,
        List<SObject> oldlist, Map<ID,SObject> oldmap)
    {

        List<Opportunity> opnewlist =
            (List<Opportunity>)newlist;
        List<Opportunity> opoldlist =
            (List<Opportunity>)oldlist;
        Map<ID, Opportunity> opnewmap =
            (Map<ID,Opportunity>)newmap;
        Map<ID, Opportunity> opoldmap =
            (Map<ID,Opportunity>)oldmap;

        // Do some processing here
        // Add entries to the dispatcher static
        // variable if they need to be updated or
        // do direct DML

    }


    public void InProgressEntry(String TriggerObject,
        Boolean IsBefore, Boolean IsDelete,
        Boolean IsAfter, Boolean IsInsert,
        Boolean IsUpdate, Boolean IsExecuting,
        List<SObject> newlist, Map<ID, SObject> newmap,
        List<SObject> oldlist, Map<ID,SObject> oldmap)

    {
```

```
    // Be sure to detect for the objects you
    // actually want to handle.
}
```

The first thing the MainEntry function is likely to do is cast the list back to the correct object type. This is safe to do because you should only call the MainEntry function with object types that can be handled by the function.

In this example, the InProgressEntry function does nothing – effectively ignoring any triggers resulting from DML operations performed in the MainEntry function (or functions it calls).

But what if you do want to execute functionality from those other triggers under some circumstances? For example: let's say you do want to allow the after-insert trigger to execute when you do an Account update DML operation.

You can modify the InProgressEntry function as follows:

```
public void InProgressEntry(String TriggerObject,
    Boolean IsBefore, Boolean IsDelete,
    Boolean IsAfter, Boolean IsInsert,
    Boolean IsUpdate, Boolean IsExecuting,
    List<SObject> newlist, Map<ID, SObject> newmap,
    List<SObject> oldlist, Map<ID,SObject> oldmap)

{
    // Be sure to detect for the objects you
    // actually want to handle.
    // Can dispatch to other classes is necessary

    // Here's how:

    if(TriggerObject == 'Account' && IsAfter)
    {
```

```
TriggerArchitectureMain1.activefunction =
    new ClassThatImplementsAccountTrigger();
TriggerArchitectureMain1.activefunction.
    MainEntry(TriggerObject, IsBefore,
    IsDelete, IsAfter, IsInsert, IsUpdate,
    IsExecuting, newlist, newmap, oldlist,
    oldmap);
TriggerArchitectureMain1.activefunction = this;
    }
}
```

When a trigger comes in that is the type you want to forward, reset the dispatch activefunction variable to the class you are about to call. Then just forward the trigger information to MainEntry method for that class. It will process the trigger as if it came in directly.

Let's take another look at what this approach really means from an architectural perspective. In traditional (simple) Force.com applications, you build a trigger by stating: "When the following database operations occurs, execute code that implements some desired functionality". This is illustrated in figure 6-5.

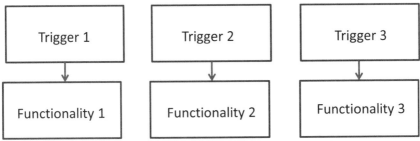

Figure 6-5 – Functionality is tied directly to a trigger

The functionality defined for each trigger is executed every time the trigger is invoked. However, that functionality might include other DML operations that in turn cause other triggers and workflows to execute – triggers and workflows that are completely out of your control. As a result, the real behavior of your application is not only unpredictable, it can vary as the system changes. The application is, as a result, extremely fragile over time.

The only way to address this is to change the original statement into a question: "I have some functionality that I wish to execute at certain times – when should I execute it?"

Your question as a developer is now: where do you answer that question?

In the TriggerArchitectureMain1.Entry3 example, the question is answered in the main dispatcher –when the trigger occurs. This is illustrated in Figure 6-6. Each trigger is responsible for deciding what functionality needs to be called. As you add more and more complexity to the system, the conditions that have to be evaluated by the triggers, or the main dispatcher for the triggers, become increasingly complex. Every time you add a DML statement any-where in your code, you need to go back to the trigger code or dispatcher to decide what to do with any triggers that may result from that DML statement.

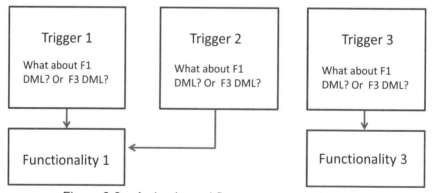

Figure 6-6 – A simple workflow can cause unintended consequences

The interface based approach simply redefines where you answer the question of when you should execute a given set of functionality. Instead of centralizing the decision, it starts with the basic assumption that if any code performs a DML operation, that code should have the right to determine how any of the triggers or workflows caused by that DML operation should be handled. So the central dispatcher need only ask the question: "Was this DML operation caused by our application?" If so, dispatch the resulting triggers to the functional block that originated the DML operation as shown in figure 6-7.

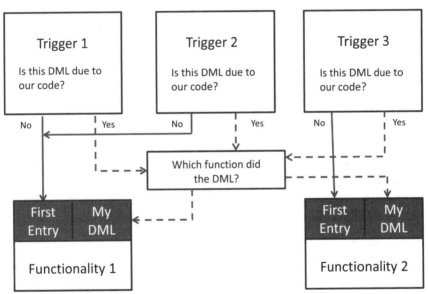

Figure 6-7– The execution decision lies with the originating functionality

Where this approach really shines over the previous one is the impact it has on the long term stability and maintainability of the application. Where before, adding any new DML operation to the code requires that you review and potentially modify the main decision code, now adding a new DML operation is perfectly safe – by default any resulting triggers or workflows will have no impact on the application because they will be quietly redirected to the originating code. On a project with multiple developers, or an application that evolves over time, this dramatically reduces the chance of errors and unintended side effects, resulting in a much more stable application.

Now I'd like you to think for a moment about the ramifications of what is possible using this architecture.

- You now have absolute and total control over the sequence of operations within your application. You also know exactly when a trigger is caused by your application, or by some outside code. This is far more detailed information than provided by the isExecuting trigger context variable.

- You now have additional information in one central location as to what your code is doing. You'll see later how this can become very useful for diagnostics and for debugging.

- Code within triggers is difficult to refactor – the only way for a trigger to invoke code in another trigger is through a DML operation. With this architecture, refactoring trigger functionality is easy, and it's trivial for one "trigger function" to call another.

- Because you can create instances of "trigger" classes directly, you can simulate trigger functionality without actually performing a DML operation. That can offer additional flexibility when testing.

- Instead of using a single static variable to track the currently executing function, you can use a list to implement stack functionality. Later in this book you'll learn how to use a variation on this technique to implement a simple execution stack trace that can be invaluable for debugging – especially with managed packages.

- With all of your trigger functionality going through one central point, you can build a centralized exception handler. You'll learn later how this can dramatically improve your ability to monitor, diagnose and support your software, and improve your users' experience.

This example is a relatively simple implementation of a centralized architecture. There are numerous ways you can build on the concepts shown here. For example:

- Your classes have entry points for the initial trigger and for "in progress" triggers. Why not an entry point for asynchronous and batch operations as well? This can dramatically simplify the effort required should you find later that you need to move some of your trigger functionality into a future call.

- Is there functionality that is common to many of your classes? Instead of an interface, consider using inheritance, where the base class implements the shared functionality and you use overrides for the MainEntry and InProgress functions.

- Remember that you are now using class instances to implement functionality instead of static methods. That means you can use constructors and properties to pass additional information to the class instances before or during processing. You can use multiple constructors depending on whether the class is being created by the main dispatch function, a future function or a batch function.

- You can create hybrid approaches, where most of your trigger functionality is handled by dispatching execution to trigger classes, but selected triggers that you want to always handle a certain way are processed separately. Think of these as "always process" conditions. By incorporating that logic into the main dispatcher, you still have complete control over the order of execution.

As you continue reading, you'll find numerous examples of the benefits of choosing a software architecture that moves trigger code into classes and uses some form of centralized dispatching.

But does it make sense to do this for quick and simple triggers? Let's face it, most Apex development is not part of an application, but rather a series of small triggers and classes that evolve over time. Can you justify the investment to build a centralized framework?

Yes – as long as you keep the framework simple. If you are a member of a team, you may be able to sell the rest of the team on using this approach once they see its value. If you are a lone consultant, who is called in periodically when work is needed, build a simple framework so you can at least manage your own code.

But if you are creating a large application or package, take the time upfront to design a solid architecture that is right for your application and build the corresponding framework. It will pay for itself many times over by simplifying your application and making it easier to understand, debug, maintain and support.

Detecting Field Changes

One of the most common design patterns in triggers involves performing an operation when a field value has changed. On the surface, this is very simple.

Consider a scenario where you want to create a task when the probability of an opportunity changes from 10 to any higher number. You might implement this functionality using a method that would be called during an after-update trigger such as the AfterUpdateOpportunityCreateTask1 method shown here:

```
public static void
    AfterUpdateOpportunityCreateTasks1(
```

```
    List<Opportunity> newlist, Map<ID, Opportunity> newmap,
    Map<ID, Opportunity> oldmap)
{
    List<Task> newtasks = new List<Task>();

    for(Opportunity op: newlist)
    {
        system.debug('old probability ' +
        oldmap.get(op.id).Probability +
        ' new probability ' + op.Probability);
        if(oldmap.get(op.id).Probability == 10
            && op.Probability > 10)
        {
            newtasks.add(new Task(ownerid = op.OwnerID,
                WhatID = op.id, ActivityDate =
                Date.Today().addDays(2),
                Subject='Opportunity stage update',
            Type='Other'));
        }
    }
        insert newtasks;
}
```

This is a standard bulk implementation of a solution to this kind of problem. And if you were a consultant building a solution for a particular organization, that would be the end of the story. All that is left is to build some test methods, one of which is shown here:

```
private static final Integer NumberOfOpportunities = 5;

static testMethod void TestTaskCount() {
    List<Opportunity> ops = new List<Opportunity>();

    for(Integer x=0; x<NumberOfOpportunities; x++)
    {
        ops.add(new Opportunity(CloseDate =
```

```
      Date.Today().addDays(5), Name = 'optest_' +
      String.valueOf(x), StageName = 'Prospecting' ));
  }
  insert ops;

  for(Opportunity op: ops)
  {
      op.StageName = 'Negotiation/Review';
  }
  Test.StartTest();
  update ops;
  Test.StopTest();

  Map<ID, Opportunity> opmap = new Map<ID, Opportunity>(ops);
  List<task> tasks = [Select ID, WhatID from
          Task where WhatID in :opmap.keyset()
          And Subject ='Opportunity stage update'];
  System.AssertEquals(NumberOfOpportunities, tasks.size());
}
```

Let's turn our attention for a moment to the workflow shown in Figure 6-8.

This workflow checks for a probability increase from 10% every time a record is changed. A field update then sets the NextStep field to a specified value.

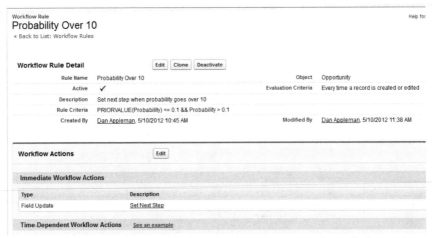

Figure 6-8 – A simple workflow can cause unintended consequences

What happens to the original solution if someone activates this workflow?

You'll get two tasks on each opportunity, and the test will fail.

The reason why this happens is subtle and is shown in Figure 6-9. The first time through the trigger, the old probability value is shown as 10 and the new value as 90 (as specified in the test code).

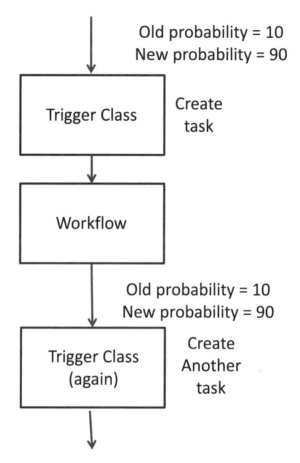

Figure 6-9 – Trigger object fields are not updated between trigger invocations

Logically, you might expect that the second time through the trigger the old value of the probability would be 90 - taking on the new value from the first time through. But in fact, the old trigger value remains the same – it reflects the field value at the start of the execution context.

When the workflow field update causes another trigger invocation, the code sees this as another field change, and creates another task.

A bit of defensive programming can avoid this problem. A simple solution might be to use a static variable to keep track of whether a task has already been created in this execution context, and simply exit if that static variable is set. However, that solution would not work in cases where it is the workflow itself that is doing a field update that you want to detect.

A more robust solution is to keep track of the correct "old" value – the value that was set during the previous trigger invocation.

```
private static Map<ID, Double>
   ProbabilityOverrides = null;

public static void
   AfterUpdateOpportunityCreateTasks2(
   List<Opportunity> newlist, Map<ID, Opportunity>
   newmap, Map<ID, Opportunity> oldmap)
{
   List<Task> newtasks = new List<Task>();
   if(ProbabilityOverrides==null)
      ProbabilityOverrides = new Map<ID, Double>();

   for(Opportunity op: newlist)
   {
      Double oldprobability =
         (ProbabilityOverrides.containskey(op.id))?
         ProbabilityOverrides.get(op.id) :
         oldmap.get(op.id).Probability;
      system.debug('old probability ' +
         oldmap.get(op.id).Probability +
         ' new probability ' + op.Probability);
      if(oldprobability == 10 && op.Probability > 10)
      {
         newtasks.add(new Task(ownerid = op.OwnerID,
            WhatID = op.id, ActivityDate =
            Date.Today().addDays(2),
```

```
                Subject='Opportunity stage update',
                Type='Other'));
      }
      if(oldprobability != op.Probability)
          ProbabilityOverrides.put(op.id, op.Probability);


   }
   insert newtasks;
}
```

The ProbabilityOverrides map keeps track of whether a previous invocation of the trigger has set a probability value. Instead of just using the value from the trigger.old context variable, the routine first checks if there is an entry in the ProbabilityOverrides map, and if so, uses that value instead.

Additional Trigger Considerations

Here are a few additional issues and best practices related to triggers of which you should be aware.

Before vs. After Triggers

It is generally better to use before triggers where possible. The biggest advantage of before triggers is that any field changes you make to an object do not require a SOQL or DML operation – so they are easier on limits. In addition, during a before operation, you have access to all of the object's fields, so you don't have to keep track of the fields you are using and make sure they are included in the SOQL query.

Use after triggers when you need to make sure that any related records (lookups, etc.) are set after an insert or update. For example: when an Opportunity is created off of a Contact record, the

OpportunityContactRole for that contact is only available during the after-insert trigger.

By the same token, use a before-delete trigger to be able to access existing related records (lookups, etc.) before they are deleted or reparented.

Always use after triggers to detect on lead conversion. Depending on the lead settings, the before triggers may not even fire.

Missing Triggers

Before designing a solution based on triggers, make sure the triggers you want to use actually exist and fire. I already noted that before triggers may not fire on conversion depending on the lead settings. If you are a consultant, you can decide that the organization turn on those triggers and validation. However, if you are creating a package, you should not require this, and should be sure your application works with conversion before-triggers and validation turned off (though you should be sure to test your code both ways).

Some objects, such as the OpportunityContactRole object, have no triggers.

Delete triggers typically do not fire on cascade deletes. If you need to detect deletion of the child objects, you must create a before-delete trigger on the parent object and perform your desired operation on the child objects at that time (be sure to design this carefully – there may be a large number of child objects).

Reparenting of objects during a merge or conversion may not fire update or delete triggers. If you merge two contacts that each have a CampaignMember object to the same campaign, one of them will vanish without triggering a deletion.

Be sure to prototype and test your scenario sufficiently to make sure that the triggers work the way you expect before investing in a full implementation.

Beware of recursion – triggers or workflows that make changes that cause another trigger invocation. The Force.com platform will only let them go to a certain level, after which the triggers will simply not fire. This will rarely be a problem if you use a centralized trigger architecture such as that described in this chapter, as it lends itself to both minimizing the number of DML operations, and to ignoring subsequent trigger invocations.

7 – Going Asynchronous

In Chapter 4, you saw a very basic asynchronous (future) pattern, and how it could be used to defer the processing of an operation on a set of objects in order to overcome limits within an Execution context. In this chapter, we'll take that basic concept, and see how far it can be extended.

Consider a scenario where you are building a knowledge base using Solution objects, and wish to add a field that contains the machine translation of the solution details, say, to Spanish. You want to build an application that will automatically populate a new custom field, SolutionSpanish__c, on insertion or update of the Solution object. To perform the translation, you'll use an external web service, such as Google Translate or Microsoft Translate.

This scenario introduces two new limits. First, you can't actually make a callout to a web service during a trigger. Second, you are limited in the number of callouts that you can make during a single execution context.

But don't let the fact that we are dealing with callout limits mislead you. The design patterns used to address these limits are exactly the same as those you would use to address other types of limits. The fact that they are more restrictive than most other limits only makes it easier to illustrate the approach.

Setting the Stage

Let's start by taking a look at the callout itself. Or rather, by the way that I'm going to cheat with regards to the callout.

My first thought was to actually implement the translation. But Google Translate costs money, and Microsoft Translate requires a

signup process – both of which are relatively easy and well docu-
mented, but would impose an annoying burden on readers. More
important, the pages it would take to describe how to do this have
nothing to do with the question at hand – that of asynchronous
design patterns. So I decided to cheat and use the following simu-
lation:

```
public class SimulatedLimitException
    extends Exception
{}


// Code to simulate a translation callout
private static Integer calloutcounter = 0;
public static string SimulateTranslationCallout(
                        String TextToTranslate)
{
    if(!System.isFuture() && ! System.isBatch()
        && !System.isScheduled()) throw new
        SimulatedLimitException('Synchronous callouts
            are not allowed within a trigger context');
    if(calloutcounter>= Limits.getLimitCallouts())
        throw new SimulatedLimitException(
                    'No more than '
                    + Limits.getLimitCallouts() +
                    ' simulated callouts allowed');
    calloutcounter+=1;
    if(TextToTranslate==null) return null;
    return TextToTranslate + ' in Spanish';
}
```

The SimulateTranslationCallout function will raise an exception if
called within a trigger context, or if called more than the number
of times allowed by the callout limits. As such, it allows us to simulate the behavior of a callout without the hassle of actually
implementing one.

A Simple (but Flawed) Implementation

The first step in the implementation should be familiar by now. We need a simple trigger that will call a class method. In this case we'll trigger both on insert and on update. Translation needs to occur on every insert, and on those updates where the Solution-Note field is changed.

```
trigger SolutionTrigger1 on Solution (after insert,
                                      after update) {
    GoingAsync.GoingAsync1(trigger.new, trigger.newmap,
        trigger.oldmap, trigger.isInsert);
}
```

You may be wondering, why use an after trigger here instead of a before trigger? In this implementation, it's necessary to use an after-insert trigger because we need an ID as a parameter to the future call. It doesn't matter for the update trigger.

Here's the GoingAsync class (that handles the trigger processing for this first attempt).

```
private static Boolean AlreadyProcessed = false;// Simple
protection from workflows and triggers

public static void GoingAsync1(List<Solution>
    solutionlist, Map<ID, Solution> newmap,
    Map<ID, Solution> oldmap, Boolean isInsert)
{
    if(AlreadyProcessed) return;
    AlreadyProcessed = true;
    if(isInsert) FirstAttempt(newmap.keyset());
    else
    {
        Set<ID> textchangedids = new Set<ID>();
```

```
    for(Solution sl: solutionlist)
    {
        if(sl.SolutionNote!= oldmap.get(sl.id).SolutionNote)
            textchangedids.add(sl.id);
    }
    if(textchangedids.size()>0)
        FirstAttempt(textchangedids);
}
}
```

This code is very straightforward. The AlreadyProcessed static variable is a simple flag to prevent reentrance due to an external workflow or trigger. Since it's unlikely a workflow would be used to modify the solution text, it should be safe to use a single gating flag instead of a flag for each individual Solution object in a batch.

For insert triggers, all of the records are processed. For update triggers, only those with changed SolutionName fields are processed.

The FirstAttempt future method is defined as follows:

```
@future
public static void FirstAttempt(Set<ID> solutionids)
{
    List<Solution> solutionstoupdate = [SELECT ID,
            SolutionNote, SolutionSpanish__c from
            Solution where ID in :solutionids];
    for(Solution sl: solutionstoupdate)
        sl.SolutionSpanish__c =
        SimulateTranslationCallout(sl.SolutionNote);
    update solutionstoupdate;
}
```

As you can see, it queries the inserted or modified solutions, performs the simulated callout, and updates the solutions with the translated text.

The TestSolutionsInsert test class validates the functionality:

```apex
private static Integer BulkTestSize = 2;

static testMethod void TestSolutionsInsert() {

    List<Solution> sols = new List<Solution>();

    for(Integer x = 0; x<BulkTestSize; x++)
    {
        sols.add(new Solution(SolutionName='solution_'
        + String.valueOf(x), Status = 'Draft',
        SolutionNote = 'This is solution # ' +
        String.ValueOf(x) ));
    }
    Test.StartTest();
    insert sols;
    Test.StopTest();

    Map<ID, Solution> solsmap = new Map<ID,
        Solution>(sols);

    List<Solution> results = [Select ID, SolutionNote,
        SolutionSpanish__c from Solution where ID in
        :solsmap.keyset()];
    for(Solution sol: results)
        System.AssertEquals(sol.SolutionNote +
            ' in Spanish', sol.SolutionSpanish__c);
}
```

You'll see that this code validates perfectly as is. But what happens if you increase the BulkTestSize variable to 11?

You'll see the simulated error:

"GoingAsync.SimulatedLimitException: No more than 10 simulated callouts allowed".

At which point you hit a dead end.

You can't start another future call from within a future call. If you just stop processing at ten callouts, you'll lose the list of solutions that still needs to be processed. And limiting the application to handling no more than ten items in a batch is just not an option.

In short, this design pattern (passing a set of object IDs to process in a future call), though common, is fundamentally flawed.

Industrial Strength Future Calls

When looking for solutions to the previous approach, you might have thought about the possibility of storing a list of those solution objects that could not be processed somewhere for later use. If so, your instincts are good. But the answer isn't to just store a list of unprocessed objects when the limit is reached. Rather, it is to always store the complete list of objects that need to be translated. And the place to do this is in a custom field on the Solution object that we'll call TranslationPending___c.

On the trigger side, the code is going to be even simpler than before. The trigger itself is changed to use before triggers, because that will make it easy to set the TranslationPending___c flag. We also get rid of the newmap parameter as it is no longer needed.

```
trigger SolutionTrigger1 on Solution (before insert,
        before update) {
    GoingAsync.GoingAsync2(trigger.new,
        trigger.oldmap, trigger.isInsert);
}
```

The GoingAsync2 function is also simpler than its predecessor. It just sets the TranslationPending__c flag for each object that is inserted or has a change to the SolutionNote field, then requests an asynchronous operation.

```
public static void GoingAsync2(List<Solution>
    solutionlist, Map<ID, Solution> oldmap,
    Boolean isInsert)
{
    if(AlreadyProcessed) return;
    AlreadyProcessed = true;
    for(Solution sl:solutionlist)
    {
        if(isInsert || sl.SolutionNote!=
            oldmap.get(sl.id).SolutionNote)
            sl.TranslationPending__c = true;
    }
    SecondAttemptRequestAsync();
}
```

The single future function has been replaced by no less than three new functions as follows:

```
public static void SecondAttemptRequestAsync()
{
    SecondAttemptAsync();
}

@future
private static void SecondAttemptAsync()
{
    SecondAttemptSync();
}

public static void SecondAttemptSync()
{
    List<Solution> solutionstoupdate = [SELECT ID, SolutionNote,
```

```
    SolutionSpanish__c from Solution where LastModifiedDate >
    :DateTime.Now().addHours(-24) And
TranslationPending__c = true
    LIMIT :Limits.getLimitCallouts()];
for(Solution s1: solutionstoupdate) {
    s1.SolutionSpanish__c =
    SimulateTranslationCallout(s1.SolutionNote);
    s1.TranslationPending__c = false;
    }
update solutionstoupdate;

}
```

There's one function to request a future call, the actual future function, and then a synchronous implementation of the processing code that is called by the asynchronous function. The query uses a limits statement to retrieve no more than the number of objects that can be processed. It also includes a conditional term based on the LastModifiedDate in order to make the query selective (LastModifiedDate is an indexed field, and queries that do not include an indexed field can fail if there are large numbers of records[2]).

Why three functions? And what is the point of this approach, given that it doesn't really solve the problem? Sure there is a limit on the query so that the exception no longer occurs in large batches, and yes, you know which Solution objects still need to be translated, but you can't actually get them translated because a future call can't trigger another future call.

Or can it?

---

[2] This is not really necessary in this example, as it's hard to imagine any organization that would have tens of thousands of solutions. But making sure queries are selective when using this design pattern is a good habit to adopt.

Controlling Asynchronous Processing

It's true that a future function cannot call another future function. But that doesn't mean it can't leave a request for another future call to be processed by other code.

For example, in this scenario, what if you placed the following code at the start of every trigger and the controller of every Visual-Force page:

```
List<Solution> solutionstoupdate = [SELECT ID,
      SolutionNote, SolutionSpanish__c from Solution
      where LastModifiedDate > :DateTime.Now().addHours(-24)
      And TranslationPending__c = true LIMIT 1];
if(solutionstoupdate.size()>0)
   GoingAsync.SecondAttemptRequestAsync()
```

On any moderately busy system, this will result in a series of future calls as long as any of the Solution objects need to be translated.

Let's ignore for the moment the question of whether or not it is a good idea to throw another query into every trigger and Visual-Force controller (it isn't). Let's ignore the fact that this solution doesn't scale well if you want to use it for multiple asynchronous functions.

Consider instead how easy it can be to implement this solution if you adopted the centralized trigger handling architecture described in Chapter 6. Since all of your triggers are already going through a central dispatcher, it would be trivial to add a couple of lines of code to the dispatcher itself and call it for every trigger. You can even add a static variable flag there to make sure it is only called once for each execution context.

Conceptually, this approach is sound. But how do you implement it without the overhead of one (or more) queries? What you really need is some kind of system flag that indicates that a future call is required – something that can be efficiently tested in each trigger with minimal impact on the system.

Fortunately, the Force.com platform provides exactly the right object for this purpose: custom settings.

Create a new list custom setting called GoAsyncHelper__c with a checkbox field AsyncPending__c. You can use a single instance of this custom setting named 'default' to hold the data. This is a common design pattern for list custom settings.

All access to this custom setting will be through a single function, GetAsyncHelper. This simplifies the rest of the code by making sure that you always have access to the correct object and that it always exists.

```
public static GoAsyncHelper__c GetAsyncHelper()
{
    GoAsyncHelper__c theobject =
        GoAsyncHelper__c.getInstance('default');
    if(theobject==null)
    {
        theobject = new GoAsyncHelper__c();
        theobject.name = 'default';
        theobject.AsyncPending__c = false;
        Database.Insert(theobject);
    }
    return theobject;
}
```

Next, centralize all requests for an asynchronous operation into a single function, ThirdAttemptRequestAsync.

```
private static Boolean ThirdAttemptAsyncRequested = false;

public static void ThirdAttemptRequestAsync()
{
    GoAsyncHelper__c asynchelper = GetAsyncHelper();
    if(ThirdAttemptAsyncRequested) return;
        // Already fired a request in this context
    if(asynchelper.AsyncPending__c) return;
        // Someone already requested async operation

    asynchelper.AsyncPending__c = true;
    Database.Update(asynchelper);

    if(!System.isFuture() && !System.isBatch()
        && !System.isScheduled())
    {
        ThirdAttemptAsyncRequested = true;
        ThirdAttemptAsync();
    }
}
```

There are some subtle aspects to this function. First, note how it uses the ThirdAttemptAsyncRequested static variable to make sure that only a single future request is made in the current execution context. This eliminates redundant future calls, and reduces the chance that you'll exceed the number of future calls allowed in an execution context, even if other code on a system is making future calls as well.

The function also exits quickly if it sees that an asynchronous request has already been made. That test, against the AsyncPending__c flag, checks requests made by any execution context.

Next, the function sets the AsyncPending__c flag to true – which serves to prevent any other calls to this function (regardless of execution context) from actually making a future call.

Finally, the code makes the future call.

This may seem like a lot of extra work compared to the previous solution, but it comes with one huge benefit. This function can safely be called at any time, both from triggers and during future calls, and it can be called as many times as you wish. Regardless of when you call it, you can count on a future call eventually being made (at least it will be, once the rest of the design is complete).

The asynchronous function itself is almost identical to the previous one.

```
@future
private static void ThirdAttemptAsync()
{
    GoAsyncHelper__c asynchelper = GetAsyncHelper();
    if(asynchelper.AsyncPending__c)
    {   // Clear any pending request
        asynchelper.AsyncPending__c = false;
        Database.Update(asynchelper);
    }

    ThirdAttemptSync();
}
```

This is the only place in the code where the AsyncPending___c flag is reset. There is a subtle race condition here. What happens if other code calls the ThirdAttemptRequestAsync function between the time this function polls the GoAsyncHelper__c object and the time it resets it to false? Is it possible that the request will be lost?

Yes, but it is highly unlikely. There are two factors at play. If the ThirdAttemptRequestAsyncHelper function is called from a non-future execution context, this won't be a problem because the ThirdAttemptAsync future function will be called regardless. And it is highly unlikely that it will be called from a future Execution context because, as you will see, the system is designed to execute asynchronous operations one after the other rather than in parallel.

The last key piece of code is the function that can be called from the central trigger dispatcher or from any VisualForce controller (during a method execute when DML operations are allowed).

```
public static void ThirdAttemptAsyncSupport()
{
    if(ThirdAttemptAsyncRequested) return;
    GoAsyncHelper__c asynchelper = GetAsyncHelper();
    if(!asynchelper.AsyncPending__c) return;
    if(System.isFuture() || System.isBatch() ||
        System.isScheduled()) return;
    ThirdAttemptAsyncRequested = true;
    ThirdAttemptAsync();
}
```

This function checks if an asynchronous operation is pending and, if so, makes the call if it is safe to do so. Because it uses a custom setting, there is very little cost to using this function – just a few lines of script.

Now let's look at the function that actually does the work

```
public static void ThirdAttemptSync()
{
    List<Solution> solutionstoupdate = [SELECT ID,
        SolutionNote, SolutionSpanish__c from Solution
        where LastModifiedDate >
        :DateTime.Now().addHours(-24) And
        TranslationPending__c = true LIMIT
        :Limits.getLimitCallouts()];
    for(Solution s1: solutionstoupdate) {
```

```
      sl.SolutionSpanish__c =
          SimulateTranslationCallout(sl.SolutionNote);
          sl.TranslationPending__c = false;
      }
    update solutionstoupdate;

    if(solutionstoupdate.size()==
        Limits.getLimitCallouts())
    {

        ThirdAttemptRequestAsync();
    }
}
```

The only difference from the previous implementation is that if the maximum number of Solution objects are found, it makes a call to the ThirdAttemptRequestAsync method to request another asynchronous operation. In effect, you have an architecture where a future call can, in effect, "call" another future method.

You may have noticed that this particular solution can lead to an extra future call if the number of Solution objects is exactly equal to the number of allowed future calls. Wouldn't it be better to do another query and see if there are any objects left before deciding whether or not to request another future call?

Maybe. Maybe not. You're trading off two limits here – the number of SOQL calls allowed in an execution context against the number of future calls allowed within a 24 hour period. Either way will work.

Scaling the Design

At the beginning of this section, I asked you to *"ignore for the moment the question of whether it is a good idea to throw another query into every trigger and VisualForce controller"* and *"ignore the fact that this solution doesn't scale well if you want to use it for multiple asynchronous functions".*

How do these concerns fare with this new architecture?

Very well indeed.

The use of efficient custom settings means that checking for a pending future call in every trigger has a very low cost. And while that does address the scalability issue in part, the real win lies with another architectural choice – moving the actual functionality into a standalone (synchronous) function instead of placing it in the future function.

Why?

Consider for a moment how you would scale this implementation to support three different asynchronous functions.

Would you build separate versions of each of these functions to define an implementation such as shown in Figure 7-1? Hopefully not.

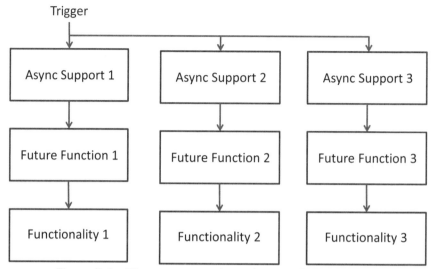

Figure 7-1 – The wrong way to scale asynchronous code

You see, in most cases your asynchronous functions won't come close to pushing the available limits. In this scenario, the future function may hit the callout limits, but is unlikely to reach the CPU timeout or SOQL limits. Wouldn't it be great to be able to perform other operations that need those limits during the same future call? Doing so could reduce further the number of future calls made, thus reducing the chance you will reach the limit on the number of future calls allowed in a 24 hour period.

Normally, you couldn't combine future call functionality in this manner because future calls can't call other asynchronous methods. But all of our functionality is implemented in regular synchronous methods, so we can implement the design pattern shown in Figure 7-2.

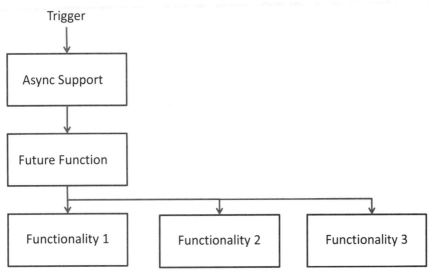

Figure 7-2 – The right way to scale asynchronous code

All you would need to do is add just a bit of intelligence to the start of each of the synchronous functions, in which it does a limit test to see if sufficient limits are available for the task at hand. In our scenario, the function might look something like this:

```
public static void ThirdAttemptSync()
{
    Integer availablecallouts =
        Limits.getLimitCallouts() -
        Limits.getCallouts();
    if(availablecallouts < 2)
    {
        ThirdAttemptRequestAsync();
        return;
    }
    List<Solution> solutionstoupdate = [SELECT ID,
        SolutionNote, SolutionSpanish__c from Solution
        where LastModifiedDate > :DateTime.Now().addHours(-24)
        And TranslationPending__c = true LIMIT
        :availablecallouts];
```

```
for(Solution sl: solutionstoupdate)
    sl.SolutionSpanish__c =
    SimulateTranslationCallout(sl.SolutionNote);
    sl.TranslationPending__c = false;
update solutionstoupdate;

if(solutionstoupdate.size()== availablecallouts)
{
    ThirdAttemptRequestAsync();
}
}
```

What you now have is, in effect, a centralized asynchronous function handler. And the benefits are far reaching:

- You can safely request asynchronous operations from anywhere in your code, including other future calls.

- You can effectively chain future calls to process larger amounts of data than you can handle in a single future call (though you'll always want to weigh the use of batch apex when you know you always need to process large amounts of data).

- Increased utilization of asynchronous execution context limits reduces the number of future calls both within an execution context and within a 24-hour period.

- Because you have stored the need for a callout on the object itself (in the TranslationPending__c field), you can extend this architecture to handle daily limits as well. You'll need to add some logic to stop making future calls when you're closing on the maximum number of calls in a 24 hour period. An additional field in the GoAsyncHelper__c object indicating that you should not actually make a future call until limits are available (at least for the translation functionality) should do the trick.

It's true that you still can't test more than ten Solution objects in your bulk unit tests. But that's a limitation of the testing framework (which can only perform one asynchronous operation in a unit test), and no longer a limitation of the architecture.

Variations

The techniques shown here for chaining future calls adapts directly to batch Apex and provides an alternative to scheduled Apex.

- Calls to your AsyncSupport function need not be limited to triggers. You can also call them from VisualForce controllers and from scheduled Apex. Just be sure to follow the scheduled Apex design patterns you'll see later in this chapter.

- On smaller organizations, triggers may not fire often enough to be of use for this pattern. In that case, consider adding a VisualForce element to frequently used page layouts, and call your async support function in the VisualForce controller. Be sure to do so during an action (action call during page load, or perhaps an actionPoller element) during which DML is allowed. Alternatively, consider combining this approach with those in the sections that follow.

Going Asynchronous with Batch Apex

When we think about batch Apex, we usually think about batch processing on existing objects. But from an execution perspective, there are many similarities between a future call and a batch execute call. You can't make a future call from a batch execute statement. You can make callouts during a batch execute statement. Each batch execute statement is asynchronous and has its own execution context. There is a limit to the number of batch execute statements that can happen in a 24 hour period.

However, unlike a future call – a batch can start another batch when it's done. It can even restart itself.

Since a batch execute statement is similar to a future call, why not use it instead of future calls?

Why not, indeed.

Let's consider a scenario similar to the one in the previous example, where we have either a callout or long-running task that needs to happen asynchronously. For example: let's say you want to use a callout to an external service to perform an address validation on every lead as it is inserted, or when its address is updated.

You could use a similar approach as before, adding a Boolean field to the lead that is queried to determine if that lead needs to be updated. But that may lead to a variety of problems. You may already be using many lead fields and your system administrators strongly oppose adding new ones. Your organization may have hundreds of thousands of leads, meaning you'd have to worry about making the queries selective, and consider the ongoing performance impact of those queries.

So let's consider a completely different approach. Since a batch execute statement is very similar to a future call, why not invoke a series of batch execute statements instead of future calls?

To do this you can create a new object – we'll call it the AsyncRequest__c object. This object has an auto-number name field, since we don't really care about the name. It has two fields. The first is a picklist called AsyncType__c that initially has one value: 'AddressVerification'. The second is a long text field called Params__c.

Class GoingAsync2 contains both the batch process implementation and some support code. Let's start by looking at some of the support code.

First there is a constant definition. The AsyncType__c field in the AsyncRequest__c object is a picklist, and it's always good to store those values in constants when doing this kind of integration – it helps prevent careless spelling errors. If the picklist value is subject to change, you would likely retrieve it using a Describe statement, but that's not necessary for this type of application where the values are hard-coded.

```
global class GoingAsync2 implements Database.Batchable<sObject>
{

    Global static final string TYPE_ADDRESSVERIFICTION =
     'AddressVerification';
```

The batch start method simply iterates over all existing AsyncRequest__c objects. The Finish method does nothing (at least for now).

```
    global Database.Querylocator Start(
```

```
            Database.BatchableContext bc)
    {
        return Database.getQueryLocator('Select ID, AsyncType__c,
                Params__c from AsyncRequest__c ');
    }
```

We'll get to the Execute and Finish methods shortly. The Start-Batch method makes it easy to start the batch.

```
    private static Boolean batchrequested = false;

    public static void StartBatch()
    {
        if(batchrequested) return;
        GoingAsync2 ga = new GoingAsync2();
        Database.executeBatch(ga, 1);
        batchrequested = true;
    }
```

There are two things to note in the StartBatch method. First, the scope on the Database.executeBatch statement is set to one. That means that each batch execute statement will be called with a single AsyncRequest__c object. In a typical batch application you want the scope to be as large as possible to take full advantage of each asynchronous execution context. But for this design pattern, we want each AsyncRequest__c object to be treated as if it were a single future call, and thus have its own execution context.

Next, we use a static Boolean variable to prevent launching the batch twice in an execution context. This makes the code more limit friendly, and because the AsyncRequest__c objects that are processed by the batch have nothing to do with the number of times the batch is started, there is no reason to ever start the batch twice in a context.

But what if the batch starts running before the execution context is finished, and more AsyncRequest__c objects are inserted during that time? The worst that will happen is they won't be picked up by this batch, but will be picked up next time it runs. And when will that be?

Take a look at the Finish statement:

```
global void Finish(Database.BatchableContext BC)
{
    List<AsyncRequest__c> ars = [Select ID
            from AsyncRequest__c Limit 1];
    if(ars.size()>0) StartBatch();
}
```

If any new AsyncRequest__c objects are inserted during the batch, this will make sure that a batch is restarted to process them.

Detecting which leads need an address verification operation starts with the OnLeadForGoingAsync2 trigger. As always, the trigger delegates its functionality to a class.

```
trigger OnLeadForGoingAsync2 on Lead (after insert,
                                after update) {
  GoingAsync2.HandleLeadTrigger(trigger.isUpdate,
            trigger.new, trigger.oldmap);
}
    public static void HandleLeadTrigger(Boolean isUpdate,
            List<Lead>newlist, Map<ID,Lead> oldmap)
    {
        List<ID> idsToProcess = new List<ID>();
        for(Lead ld: newlist)
        {
            if(!isUpdate)
            {
```

```
            idsToProcess.add(ld.id);
        }
        else
        {
            Lead oldlead = oldmap.get(ld.id);
            if(ld.city!= oldlead.city ||
                ld.street!=oldlead.street ||
                ld.state!=oldlead.state ||
                ld.country!=oldlead.country ||
                ld.postalcode!=oldlead.postalcode)
                idsToProcess.add(ld.id);
        }
    }
    if(idsToProcess.size()==0) return;
    List<AsyncRequest__c> newrequests =
        new List<AsyncRequest__c>();
    List<ID> idsForRequest = new List<ID>();
    for(ID currentid: idsToProcess)
    {
        idsForRequest.add(currentid);
        if(idsForRequest.size()==10)
        {
            newrequests.add(new AsyncRequest__c(
                AsyncType__c = TYPE_ADDRESSVERIFICTION,
                Params__c = String.Join(idsForRequest,',') ));
            idsForRequest.clear();
        }
    }
    if(idsForRequest.size()>0)
        newrequests.add(new AsyncRequest__c(
            AsyncType__c = TYPE_ADDRESSVERIFICTION,
            Params__c = String.Join(idsForRequest,',') ));
    insert newrequests;
    StartBatch();
}
```

The HandleLeadTrigger method performs two tasks. First, it figures out which leads need to be updated. This includes all newly inserted leads, and any leads with address updates.

Next it creates a series of AsyncRequest__c objects where the IDs of the leads to update are stored as a comma separated list in the Params__c field.

As you can see, this is a very efficient solution. With the exception of the String.Join method, all of the Apex statements are very simple methods and comparisons. There is just one DML statement. So even with batches of 200 leads, you are unlikely to see limit issues due to this code.

Now let's look at the batch execute method:

```
global void Execute(Database.BatchableContext BC,
                List<AsyncRequest__c> scope)
{
    List<AsyncRequest__c> objectsToDelete =
        new List<AsyncRequest__c>();
    for(AsyncRequest__c ar: scope)
    {
        // Remember, this will really only happen once
        if(ar.AsyncType__c == TYPE_ADDRESSVERIFICTION)
        {
            List<ID> idsToProcess = ar.Params__c.split(',');
            // Now do a query here agains the IDs - bad ids
            // are ok, they won't have an object
            // Do the callout, update here
            objectsToDelete.add(ar);
        }
    }
    if(objectsToDelete.size()>0)
    {
        delete objectsToDelete;
```

```
Database.emptyRecycleBin(objectsToDelete);
    }

}
```

Even though the scope of the batch was set to one, the function still uses the standard bulk pattern. This helps keep things simple and consistent, and helps avoid errors should someone accidently invoke the batch with a larger scope. The Execute statement identifies the type of AsyncRequest__c object and performs the requested operation. The Params__c field contains a list of the lead IDs to process – you will use this in a SOQL query.

What if a lead has been deleted between the time the batch was requested and the time the Execute statement is called? No problem – just be sure to perform all further work based on the records actually retrieved from the query, not those in the original parameter list. Leads for deleted Ids simply won't show up in the query.

Once the request is processed, it is usually deleted (though as you will see in chapter 8, there are cases you may not want to do so). Because large numbers of these objects might be created and deleted over time, and system administrators sometimes get annoyed when developers fill the recycled object bin with objects that will never need to be recovered, it's always nice to remove the objects from the recycle bin as well.

Now you can perform the callout and any long operations you wish.

You might be wondering, why have the AsyncType__c field at all?

Well, what would it take to move the previous example, of translating solutions, into this approach? I think you'll agree it would be quite straightforward. But the last thing you'd want to do is define separate request objects for address verification and solution translation – that would be a waste of an object. Instead, you could just define a new picklist value in the AsyncType__c field, and a new constant in the GoingAsync2 class, then create the necessary setup and handler code so that the batch will happily process both types of async requests.

Come to think of it, there is no limit to the type of asynchronous operations you can define. And no need to restrict yourself to a single Parameter field – you can define additional fields on the AsyncRequest__c object that work with specific types of requests.

In short, this design pattern isn't about address verification at all – rather, it represents the foundation of an approach that can be used to turn almost any operation into an asynchronous operation. And since you can insert a very large number of AsyncRequest__c objects with a single DML operation, you can effectively start a lot more than the 10 future operations allowed within an execution context. Given that you can define all kinds of fields on the AsyncRequest__c object, you have vastly greater flexibility with regards to the amount of data you can pass to the asynchronous operation as well.

This design pattern is also very resistant to exceptions. If an exception occurs in a future call, any information about the call, such as the parameters for the call, will likely be lost unless you have good data logging in place. They'll certainly be lost if it's a limit issue, as many limit exceptions stop execution without the possibility of logging any data.

But if an exception occurs during a batch execute statement, it may terminate that one execution. It may even terminate the entire batch. But the original AsyncRequest__c object will still be there – it doesn't get deleted until the operation has been completed successfully.

Of course this opens the possibility of a bad request that leads to an endless series of exceptions and return attempts that can cause you to exceed your allowed number of future calls in a 24 hour period. So you should definitely include robust error handling – more robust than shown here. For example: what if some fool hand edits an AsyncRequest__c record to place data in the Params__c field that can't be converted into an ID? This example will blow up nicely.

There is one catch to using batch Apex to replace future calls. While it is true that there is no guarantee as to when a future or batch call will execute, future calls do tend to execute very soon after they are requested, whereas batch calls, depending on system load, tend to have longer delays before they start. It's never a good idea to assume that any asynchronous operation will occur in a given amount of time, but this is a factor to consider in your design.

One last note: There's an inefficiency in this implementation that could cause a lead to be processed for verification more than once. Do you see it? How would you address it? [Hint – it's discussed in the previous chapter].

Going Asynchronous with Scheduled Apex

In the previous example, the batch is executed almost any time AsyncRequest__c objects are inserted. This is potentially a problem. You might end up with two or more batches running at once. This could lead to concurrency issues (a topic I'll cover in the next chapter). You may end up running your asynchronous processing code more often than you need to. In many cases it's fine to wait a few minutes, if not a few hours, for an asynchronous operation to occur.

One way to address this problem, that also opens up an entirely new set of interesting possibilities, involves the use of Scheduled Apex.

In the past, it was advisable to avoid using scheduled Apex. This is because when you have a class scheduled using scheduled Apex, it is impossible to update that class. The class is locked because the platform internally stores a serialized instance of that class. Worse, the platform also prevents updates to any classes that are referenced by the scheduled class. This means that many of your code updates require the additional step of deleting any scheduled jobs and then restarting them after the update.

The problem is even worse if you are building an AppExchange package. It can make it virtually impossible to push patches and updates to your users.

Fortunately, recent changes to Apex have enabled a design pattern that can allow you to use scheduled Apex without facing this problem. The idea is to create a simple Apex class that is schedulable, that will call into other code, but not reference that code. This schedulable class will be locked when scheduled, but it won't lock any other code in your application. With luck, it will never need to be updated. What's more, package installations and upgrades are intelligent enough to recognize that a class has not changed, and will not attempt to update it – thus the fact that the class is locked will not interfere with package deployments and push updates.

The ScheduledDispatcher class demonstrates this principle.

```
global class ScheduledDispatcher Implements Schedulable {
    public Interface IScheduleDispatched
    {
        void execute(SchedulableContext sc);
    }
```

```
global void execute(SchedulableContext sc)
{
    Type targettype =
        Type.forName('GoingAsync2.ScheduleHandler');
    if(targettype!=null) {
        IScheduleDispatched obj =
            (IScheduleDispatched)targettype.NewInstance();
        obj.execute(sc);
    }
}
}
```

The class defines an interface that can be referenced by another class. When the system scheduler calls the execute method, the code uses the Type.forName method to first obtain the type object for the class that will implement the desired functionality, then uses the NewInstance method to create an instance of that class. As long as the class implements the IScheduleDispatched interface, you will be able to call its execute method.

In this example, the delegated class is an inner class in the GoingAsync2 class called ScheduleHandler. In this example, the scheduled operation starts the GoingAsync2 batch and aborts the scheduled job. You'll see why, shortly.

```
public class ScheduleHandler
    implements ScheduledDispatcher.IScheduleDispatched
{
    public void execute(SchedulableContext sc)
    {
        StartBatch();
        system.abortJob(sc.getTriggerID());
        // Always abort the job on completion
    }
}
```

Scheduler Ping-Pong

In the existing GoingAsync2 sample code, each call to the Start-Batch method would start a new batch. Given that the batch can support many types of asynchronous requests, it stands to reason that requests to start the batch may come from many places in the code. As mentioned earlier, this can result in numerous batches running concurrently as shown in figure 7-3, potentially exceeding limits or leading to other concurrency issues.

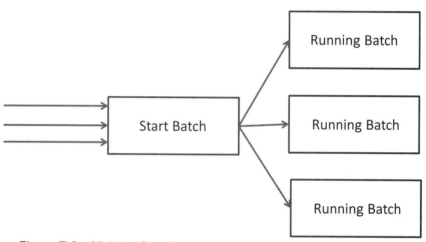

Figure 7-3 – Multiple StartBatch requests results in multiple batches

One way to avoid this is to use the Apex scheduler to control batch execution. The idea is that instead of calling the StartBatch method to start the batch execution, you would call a StartScheduler method, and run the batch when the scheduled event occurs as shown in figure 7-4.

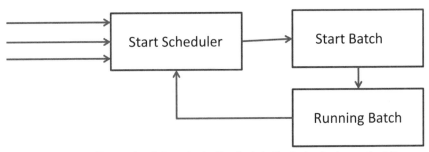

Figure 7-4 – The scheduler starts the batch that can in turn start the scheduler

This scenario is implemented in the GoingAsync2 StartScheduler method.

```
public static void StartScheduler()
{
    // Consider putting a static variable gate here so the
    // method is only called once per execution context
    // (like StartBatch)

    // Is the job already running?
    List<CronTrigger> jobs = [SELECT Id, CronJobDetail.Name,
    State, NextFireTime FROM CronTrigger
    where CronJobDetail.Name='async2_example_job'];
    if(jobs.size()>0 && jobs[0].state!='COMPLETED' &&
            jobs[0].state!='ERROR' && jobs[0].state!='DELETED')
    {
        // It's already running - Is the batch running?
        Set<String> activejobstates =
            new Set<String>{'Queued','Processing','Preparing'};
        List<AsyncApexJob> apexjobs = [Select ID, ApexClass.Name
                from AsyncApexJob where
                ApexClass.Name = 'GoingAsync2' And
                Status in :activejobstates];
        if(apexjobs.size()>0) return;// The batch is running
        // If we're going to run soon, exit
        if(DateTime.Now().AddSeconds(60) > jobs[0].NextFireTime)
```

```
        return;

    }

    // If the job exists, it needs to be deleted
    if(jobs.size()>0) system.abortJob(jobs[0].id);

    // Instead of 10 seconds, you could query pending async
    // requests to decide a target time
    try {
        System.schedule('async2_example_job',
                    GetSchedulerExpression(
                    DateTime.Now().addSeconds(10)),
                    new ScheduledDispatcher());
    } catch(Exception ex){}
}
```

When the StartScheduler function is called, it first determines if the scheduled job already exists. If so, it checks if the asynchronous batch is running or if the scheduled job is going to fire very soon. In either case, the request is ignored, as asynchronous processing is either underway or will soon commence.

If the scheduled job exists but is set to fire too far in the future, the existing job is aborted.

Finally, a new Apex job is scheduled to run. The System.Schedule call is placed in an exception block to handle the unlikely (but possible) case where two threads attempt to start the scheduler at exactly the same time. The platform will see that job 'async2_example_job' already exists, and the second attempt will fail with an error. This error can be ignored because the only thing we care about is that the job is scheduled.

When the scheduled job executes, the asynchronous batch is started and the job is aborted as you've seen in the ScheduleHandler execute method.

```
public void execute(SchedulableContext sc)
{
    StartBatch();
    system.abortJob(sc.getTriggerID());
    // Always abort the job on completion
}
```

All of the code that used to call the StartBatch method in the previous example, including the HandleLeadTrigger method and the batch Finish method, is changed to call StartScheduler instead.

Now you can safely call StartScheduler at any time, knowing that it will only create the Scheduled Apex job if necessary. It will start the GoingAsync2 batch at the scheduled time, and that batch will recreate the Scheduled Apex job if necessary.

Variations

You may have noticed in the code that the StartScheduler method always sets the scheduler to start in 10 seconds. This makes sense for cases where you want to run the asynchronous operation as soon as possible. But it also opens the possibility to an even more flexible solution. What if you added a target time field to the AsyncRequest__c object specifying when you want that object to be processed? You could then add a condition to the query in the batch start method to only iterate over those AsyncRequest__c objects that are at or past their target time. The StartScheduler method could then query the AsyncRequest__c table to find the earliest target time and use that as the fire time for the Scheduled Apex job instead of ten seconds.

You would then have a highly flexible scheduling system, that allows you to schedule as many asynchronous operations as you wish, for exactly the times you desire. And it only uses a single scheduled Apex job!

8 – Concurrency

There are two errors possible in APEX that many developers will never see. The first is:

```
EXCEPTION_THROWN [32]|System.QueryException: Record Currently
Unavailable: The record you are attempting to edit, or one of
its related records, is currently being modified by another
user. Please try again.
```

The second is:

```
FATAL_ERROR System.DmlException: Update failed. First exception
on row 0 with id ...............; first error: UNABLE_TO_LOCK_ROW, unable
to obtain exclusive access to this record: []
```

If you have never seen either of these errors, count yourself lucky. I encourage you to read this chapter regardless. It will help you to design more robust code should you ever find yourself having to implement an application that demands a high degree of reliability and fault tolerance. And it will help you to avoid panic should you run into either of these errors in the future.

If you have run into either of these errors, I think you will find this chapter helpful.

Introduction to Concurrency

If you come to Apex from another language, you are likely already familiar with the concept of concurrency from your experience with multithreading. Then again, I have met a fair number of developers who use languages that support multithreading, who don't really understand the nature of what they are dealing with. So, for the benefit of those who don't have extensive experience with the topic, I'm going to take a somewhat more introductory approach here than I have in other chapters.

The problem of concurrency in real life may be quite familiar to you. Let's say that you and your spouse have a joint checking account with a balance of $100. You're both shopping for gifts for the holidays. You find the perfect gift, and just to be safe, check your account balance and confirm that it is indeed $100. Knowing this, you confidently write a check for $75 for your gift. At exactly the same moment, your spouse does exactly the same thing.

Both of you "know" that you have a balance of $100. So each of you spends $75, confident that the checks are good. But together you've spent $150 and one of those checks is going to bounce.

This is a classic concurrency problem. It can happen any time that two separate operations are able to access a shared resource.

Of all the software bugs that are possible, none are harder to solve than concurrency problems.

Here's why.

What are the chances that two sales reps will happen to be modifying the exact same field on the same object at the same time? What are the chances that two asynchronous processes or incoming service calls will do the same? On a smaller or lower traffic system, the odds might be a million to one against. So a concurrency related bug might only happen once every few years.

How do you detect, reproduce and debug a problem that occurs so infrequently? It's virtually impossible.

In many applications, when these problems do occur, they aren't even recognized. Someone notices some data that is incorrect and assumes it was edited in error. In many cases it's not a big deal. But if you're building a financial application, these errors can be serious – money can literally appear or disappear, seemingly at random.

The cost to identify concurrency bugs, reproduce them, and fix them, can be virtually unlimited. The only real way to address concurrency issues is at design time.

From a language perspective, Apex is not a multithreaded language. There is no shared data. There is no ability to create traditional threads. All static variables are the equivalent of what in the multithreading world is called "thread local storage" – they are specific to one thread and one execution context.

However, Force.com asynchronous processes do run in separate threads and can be concurrent. And those processes can access the database. So concurrency issues can occur – especially on high traffic systems, or systems that support many asynchronous processes or incoming service calls.

For this reason, it is essential that you understand concurrency and how to deal with it in your code.

Optimistic Concurrency

Let's examine a concurrency scenario from the Salesforce world.

Imagine a $20,000 opportunity that has two related contacts. Each contact is working with a separate sales person. At exactly the same time each contact calls their sales rep and gives them the good news – they're going to spend an extra $10,000 as shown in figure 8-1.

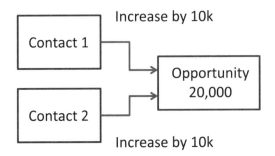

Figure 8-1 – Two contacts each increase an opportunity by 10K

The sales reps, thrilled, immediately go to their computers. On seeing that the current value of the opportunity is 20K, they edit the opportunity and set it to 30K as shown in figure 8-2.

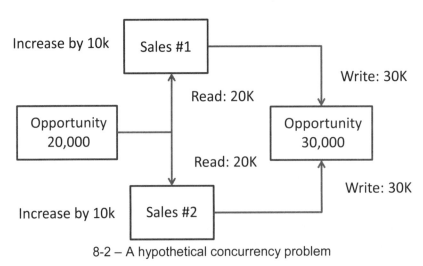

8-2 – A hypothetical concurrency problem

Because each sales person sees the current value as 20K, and updates the opportunity to 30K, nobody will realize that the opportunity should have been 40K unless the sales reps happen to compare notes.

Those of you with experience with this kind of scenario might see a problem with this example. In practice, if two sales reps try to update an opportunity at once, when the second sales rep tries to save the data, an error message will be displayed in the Salesforce user interface. The error will be the first one I listed: "The record you are attempting to edit, or one of its related records, is currently being modified by another user. Please try again."

That's because the Salesforce user interface is clever and implements the scenario as shown in figure 8-3:

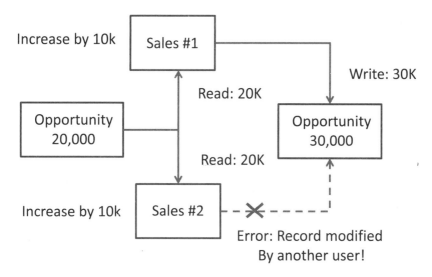

8-3 – Optimistic Record Locking

When the second user tries to update the opportunity, the system detects that the opportunity has been updated by another user since the edit session began, and blocks the update. Salesforce is using a type of record locking approach called optimistic record locking (though purists will note that this is not true optimistic locking at the database level). This approach assumes that there won't be any concurrency issues, trusting on the ability of the system to detect them and report an error when they occur.

The ability of Salesforce to detect concurrency issues is limited. For one thing, it only applies to different users. If you have two asynchronous or external service calls running in the same user context, and a concurrency issue comes up, it will typically not be detected. If Apex code modifies a record that is being edited in the user interface by a different user, Salesforce will detect that another user modified the record and report an error. However, in the unlikely event that another user modifies a record between the time your Apex code queries a record and updates it, the concurrency error will not be detected.

This means that if you are building a very high reliability application that supports asynchronous operations, you must either implement your own concurrency error detection, or use pessimistic record locking.

Pessimistic Record Locking (For Update)

For cases where you want to be certain that your execution context has sole access to a record, you can use a technique called pessimistic record locking. This is implemented by adding the "For Update" term to your SOQL query.

When you lock a record with a "for update" query, any other thread that attempts to read that record will block – it will wait until the execution context that locked the record completes. Once the first execution context is finished, the blocked thread will be allowed to continue as shown in figure 8-4. In this example, Sales rep #2 will not be able to query the opportunity until Sales rep #1 has completed editing the record.

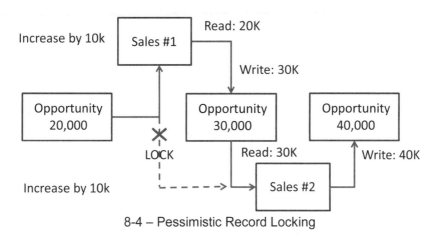

8-4 – Pessimistic Record Locking

What happens if the code processing Sales Rep #1 takes a very long time, say more than 10 seconds? At that point the block on Sales Rep #2 times out and you get the notorious UNABLE_TO_LOCK_ROW error.

In reality, it's not necessary for one process to hold a lock on a record to cause this error. If you have many processes attempting to access the same record, each one will be unblocked in turn as the previous one completes. But if any process is blocked for too long, it will time out with the UNABLE_TO_LOCK_ROW error.

One of the most common ways this can happen is if you have data skew in your organization.

For example: normally each account might have a relatively small number of contacts. But let's say that you have a "catch-all" account to hold contacts that don't have a specific account. In this case you can end up with one account with a very large number of contacts.

Any time you insert a contact or change the owner on a contact, Salesforce locks the parent account to maintain data integrity. So that catch-all account might spend quite a bit of time being locked.

Worse, those operations may involve recalculating sharing rules, which is potentially very time consuming when you have a large number of contacts. If another thread tries to update the parent account or any of its related contacts, you may see an UNABLE_TO_LOCK_ROW error.

Your Apex code also locks records in two ways. First, it locks a record when you use "For Update" in a query. Second, it locks a record when you update it. Why is this? Because if Apex code terminates with an exception, the system reverts the entire transaction. If the platform did not lock the records, other processes could modify those records and the revert operation would cause those changes to be lost without notice or warning. This lock is held until the execution context ends.

On low traffic systems, and systems with small applications, chances are good you will never see a locking error. That's because the ten second lock timeout is really a very long time. However, on high traffic systems, or systems with large applications, UNABLE_TO_LOCK_ROW errors can appear, and they can become painfully common.

There are two key design principles that you can use to minimize the chances of this error occurring even on high traffic systems:

- Avoid data skew
- Defer DML updates until near the end of the execution context

Handling DML lock errors

It is impossible to guarantee 100% that DML lock errors will not occur on a system. The question is, how should you handle them?

For synchronous operations, say triggers or UI operations, the answer is usually simple – don't handle them at all. Lock errors will be raised and the DML operations will return an error result. If it's a user operation, the user will see an error message inviting them to try again later. Any other changes made during the operation will revert and no harm will be done.

But what if the lock errors occurs during an asynchronous operation? By default, the best you can hope for is a system Apex error message that provides minimal insight as to where the errors occurred, and no information regarding the data being processed. In other words, you will see data loss – not what you want to have happen in a high reliability system.

For a high reliability system it is not enough to minimize the chances of DML lock errors – you need a detection, reporting and recovery mechanism as well. That's what we'll look at next.

Reproducing DML Lock errors

It's hard to write code for an error condition that rarely occurs. It's even harder to test it. So the first order of business in learning how to deal with these errors is to find a way to reproduce them.

Because concurrency errors involve timeouts, the first step is to find a way to create a nice long delay in Apex. Fortunately, this is not difficult. The stage was already set in chapter 3 where we discussed CPU time limits and the fact that some built-in operations can take a significant amount of time to run.

The Concurrency1.Delay class uses JSON serialization of a long array to generate a delay. The actual length of the delay will vary. Though the delay parameter is called "seconds", it's a very rough approximation. In our tests we'll use trial and error to pick numbers that are long enough to generate timeouts without exceeding CPU time limits.

```
public static void Delay(Integer seconds)
{
    List<Integer> largearray = new List<Integer>();
    for(Integer x =0; x<10000; x++) largearray.add(x);
    for(Integer counter = 0; counter<seconds * 4; counter++)
    {
        String s = json.serialize(largearray);
    }
}
```

Unlike much of the code in this book, you can't do concurrency testing in a unit test. Unit tests serialize asynchronous requests, running them all synchronously after the Test.StopTest function is called.

To use the tests that follow, you must create an opportunity named "Concurrency1"

The two main methods in the Concurrency1 class are the IncrementOptimistic and IncrementPessimistic classes.

```
// Create this opportunity by hand
private static String OpportunityName = 'Concurrency1';

@future
public static void IncrementOptimistic(double amount,
    Integer DelayBefore, Integer DelayFromQuery,
    Integer DelayAfter)
{
    if(DelayBefore>0) Delay(DelayBefore);
    List<Opportunity> ops = [Select ID, Amount From Opportunity
                    where Name = :OpportunityName];
    for(Opportunity op: ops)
        op.Amount = (op.Amount==null)? amount:
            op.Amount + Amount;
```

```
    if(DelayFromQuery>0) Delay(DelayFromQuery);
    update ops;
    if(DelayAfter>0) Delay(DelayAfter);
}


@future
public static void IncrementPessimistic(double amount,
    Integer DelayBefore, Integer DelayFromQuery,
    Integer DelayAfter)
{
    if(DelayBefore>0) Delay(DelayBefore);
    List<Opportunity> ops = [Select ID, Amount From Opportunity
                     where Name = :OpportunityName For Update];
    for(Opportunity op: ops)
       op.Amount = (op.Amount==null)? amount:
          op.Amount + Amount;
    if(DelayFromQuery>0) Delay(DelayFromQuery);
    update ops;
    if(DelayAfter>0) Delay(DelayAfter);
}
```

Both of these methods implement the following algorithm:

- Delay *DelayBefore* seconds
- Query the opportunity record
- Delay *DelayFromQuery* seconds
- Increment a field and update the opportunity record
- Delay *DelayAfter* seconds

The IncrementPessimistic method uses the "For Update" term in the query to support pessimistic record locking.

These two functions allow you to experiment and reproduce all kinds of locking scenarios. All you need to do is open an anonymous Apex window in the developer console, and execute two or more (up to ten) of these functions at once.

Let's start with some of the optimistic locking scenarios.

Open the Concurrency1 opportunity that you created and set the value in the Amount field to zero.

In your anonymous Apex window, enter:

```
Concurrency1.IncrementOptimistic(10,0,2,0);
Concurrency1.IncrementOptimistic(10,1,0,0);
```

When you execute these commands, the two future calls will start running concurrently. The first one will query the value of the amount, wait two seconds, and update the record, adding 10 to the original amount. The second method will wait one second, query the record and update it immediately, adding 10 to the original amount. You may need to repeat this test to see the results, as there is no guarantee that both future operations will start at the same time.

Both of these methods increment the Amount by ten, so one would expect the end value to be 20. But the resulting value will be only ten. You've effectively reproduced a concurrency error by stretching out the time of the operations.

Now let's reproduce a lock error.

Try executing the following in your anonymous Apex window:

```
Concurrency1.IncrementOptimistic(10,0,0,25);
Concurrency1.IncrementOptimistic(10,1,0,0);
```

The first method immediately adds 10 to the amount and updates the opportunity record. It then waits over 10 seconds before exiting (you may need to tinker with the value of the DelayAfter parameter – too short and it may not timeout, too long and you may see CPU timeout limits instead of DML lock errors).

The second method waits one second, then attempts to update the record. However, it is blocked by the first method. After about 10 seconds, the second method aborts with a DML lock (UNABLE_TO_LOCK_ROW) error.

Now let's look at a pessimistic locking example.

Reset the opportunity amount field to zero, then execute the following anonymous Apex:

```
Concurrency1.IncrementPessimistic(10,0,2,0);
Concurrency1.IncrementPessimistic(10,1,0,0);
```

This is the same scenario you saw earlier with the first optimistic locking example. But this time the amount field does increment to 20. That's because the second method call is blocked and waits until the first one completes before it reads the record. The record thus contains the value as updated by the first method call.

But what if the first method takes too long to finish and the second method is blocked for too long? You can illustrate that scenario with the following code (again, you may need to tinker with the actual timeout value).

```
Concurrency1.IncrementPessimistic(10,0,20,0);
Concurrency1.IncrementPessimistic(10,0,20,0);
```

One of the methods should fail with the following exception:

```
System.QueryException: Record Currently Unavailable: The record
you are attempting to edit, or one of its related records, is
currently being modified by another user. Please try again.
```

You can experiment with these functions to reproduce a variety of locking scenarios. You also now have a tool that can allow you to create lock errors and thus create, test and debug code designed to handle them, instead of just having to simulate those errors in unit tests.

Reprocessing DML lock errors

When you run into a DML lock error in a synchronous operation, you may prefer to just let the error occur and allow the user or caller to handle the error. But if you want to handle these errors in an asynchronous operation, you have only two options – log the error, or try to recover from the error.

In either case, the first thing you have to do is capture the error. This is done by replacing the Update statement with the following code:

```
List<Database.Saveresult> dmlresults =
    Database.Update(ops, false);
List<Opportunity> FailedUpdates = new List<Opportunity>();
for(Integer x = 0; x< ops.size(); x++)
{
    Database.Saveresult sr = dmlresults[x];
    if(!sr.isSuccess())
    {
        for(Database.Error err: sr.getErrors())
        {
            if(err.getStatusCode() ==
                StatusCode.UNABLE_TO_LOCK_ROW)
            {
                FailedUpdates.add(ops[x]);
                break;
            }
        }
    }
}
```

```
}

if(FailedUpdates.size()>0) {
    // Do a logging or recovery operation here
}
```

The Database.Update statement has a parameter *opt_allOrNone* which can be set to false to indicate that the code should return an error result rather than throwing an exception. On return, the software tests each result to see if any failed. If the failure was due to a DML lock, the opportunity is stored in an array. We set the *opt_allOrNone* false because in a bulk update it's very likely that the concurrency error would only apply to one or two records in the batch.

There are other types of DML errors that can occur here, so in a real application you might want to extend this code to detect and handle different errors. For example: while it might make sense to retry a DML failure due to a DML lock, you would likely want to log an error caused by a validation rule, as retrying it later is un-likely to work.

Things get more complex if you are updating related objects at the same time. In that case you may prefer to keep the *opt_allOrNone* field true and use the DML savepoint capability to wrap your DML operation inside of a transaction. But that's an entirely different topic, and beyond the scope of this chapter.

Logging DML lock errors in this scenario is straightforward – just use a custom object to store any failure information that you wish to track. While the opportunity record may be locked, that won't prevent you from inserting a new custom object. You'll read more about diagnostic logging in chapter 9.

The interesting thing about a DML lock error is that it is recoverable. Even though this update timed out, one would expect that at some time in the future the update will succeed. So it's quite reasonable to try again sometime in the future. Because you're in a future or batch context already, you can't just perform a future call. However, by remarkable coincidence, you already have a very nice asynchronous processing system that was implemented in chapter 7.

All it takes are a few simple changes to the AsyncType__c object:

- Add a currency field NewAmount__c
- Add a currency field OriginalAmount__c
- Add a lookup to an opportunity field TargetOpportunity__c
- Add picklist value "Amount Update" to the AsyncType__c field.

The RecordRecoveryInformation method creates a new AsyncRequest__c object for each failed opportunity:

```
private static void RecordRecoveryInformation(List<Opportunity>
            failedops, double amount)
{
    List<AsyncRequest__c> requests = new List<AsyncRequest__c>();
    for(Opportunity op: failedops)
    {
        requests.add(new AsyncRequest__c(
            AsyncType__c = GoingAsync2.TYPE_AMOUNTUPDATEFAILURE,
            NewAmount__c = op.Amount,
            OriginalAmount__c = op.Amount - amount,
            TargetOpportunity__c = op.id));
    }
    insert requests;
```

```
// Request the async operation
GoingAsync2.StartScheduler();
}
```

This method is called from the IncrementOptimisticWithCapture method as follows:

```
if(FailedUpdates.size()>0)
{
    // Do a logging or recovery operation here
    RecordRecoveryInformation(FailedUpdates, amount);
}
```

There's a bit of a "cheat" here, where I determine the original value of the opportunity by subtracting the amount that was previously added. In a real application, you would likely keep an array of original values around in case you wanted to save them when failures occur. Why save the original value? You'll see that shortly.

As you can see from the above code, a new global variable was added to the GoingAsync2 example to define the new async request type.

The GoingAsync2.Start method needs to be modified to query the new AsyncRequest__c object fields:

```
global Database.Querylocator Start(Database.BatchableContext bc)
{
    return Database.getQueryLocator('Select ID, AsyncType__c,
        Params__c, TargetOpportunity__c, NewAmount__c,
        OriginalAmount__c from AsyncRequest__c ');
}
```

Now all that remains is to modify the batch execute statement. Overall, the new function will look like this:

```
global void Execute(Database.BatchableContext BC,
                    List<AsyncRequest__c> scope)
{
    List<AsyncRequest__c> objectsToDelete =
        new List<AsyncRequest__c>();
    for(AsyncRequest__c ar: scope)
    {
        // Remember, this will really only happen once
        if(ar.AsyncType__c == TYPE_ADDRESSVERIFICTION)
        {
            List<ID> idsToProcess = ar.Params__c.split(',');
            objectsToDelete.add(ar);
        }

        if(ar.AsyncType__c == TYPE_AMOUNTUPDATEFAILURE)
        {
            Opportunity op = [Select ID, Amount from Opportunity
                where ID = :ar.TargetOpportunity__c for update];
                if(op==null) {
                    // The op may have been deleted
                    objectsToDelete.add(ar); continue;
                }
                // WHAT GOES HERE???

        }
    }
    if(objectsToDelete.size()>0)
    {
        delete objectsToDelete;
        Database.emptyRecycleBin(objectsToDelete);
    }

}
```

As you can see, adding processing for a new type of asynchronous operation is very simple. You can also see that I'm breaking the cardinal rule here – using a single object pattern instead of a bulk pattern.

Even though this subsystem is designed to only execute one object at a time, I was sorely tempted to build this using a bulk pattern - creating a separate list of opportunity IDs to query, then doing the query, then processing them one at a time and doing a final update. But the truth is that doing so would make this particular example considerably harder to read and understand.

Now comes the big question. What fits into that block titled "WHAT GOES HERE???"

Well, it depends.

You could do a simple amount update like this:

```
op.Amount = ar.NewAmount__c;
```

But there's a problem with this approach. What if somebody else has updated the opportunity amount in the meantime? In that case, you're just trading a DML lock error for a concurrency error.

You could say that what you really want to do is increment the amount field regardless of the current value. In that case you can do the following:

```
op.Amount += (ar.NewAmount__c - ar.OriginalAmount__c);
```

This avoids the concurrency error by redefining the nature of the asynchronous operation from saving a value to incrementing a value.

Another approach is to validate the current value of the opportunity against the original opportunity value – checking if some other process may have updated the amount.

```
if(op.Amount!= ar.OriginalAmount__c)
{
    // Concurrency error - log it here, don't update
    objectsToDelete.add(ar);
    continue;
}
```

What you are doing here is a very traditional form of optimistic locking – where you test to see if there is a concurrency issue before performing an update. In this case, if you see the value of the amount has changed, you can assume that there is a concurrency issue. You can then log the error and not update the opportunity.

When it comes to updating the opportunity, as hard as it is to imagine, it's still possible to run into yet another DML lock error. However, in this case it's easy enough to handle – if you see a DML lock error, just exit the routine without deleting the AsyncRequest__c object. That way, next time the async routine runs, your code will try the update again. Here's one way you can implement this:

```
try
{
    update op;
}
catch(DmlException dex)
{
    if(dex.getDmlType(0) == StatusCode.UNABLE_TO_LOCK_ROW)
    {
        continue;  // Try again later
```

```
    }
    // Otherwise log the error
}
catch(Exception ex)
{
    // Log the error?
}
objectsToDelete.add(ar);
```

Dealing with concurrency can be a huge headache. The only thing worse is not dealing with it in organizations and applications where it is really needed.

Many Apex developers can get away with ignoring this issue. It is rare on many systems. And to be perfectly honest, in many organizations the data in the org is so inaccurate anyway that an occasional undetected concurrency error will never be noticed and never matter.

But if you are building an application that demands a high level of reliability and accuracy – say, a financial application, you should at the very least be aware of potential concurrency issues, and design your application with them in mind.

Part III – Testing, Debugging and Deployment

The best design patterns, architectures, and coding practices aren't worth anything if you can't successfully deploy your application. When it comes to testing, debugging and deploying applications, the Force.com platform is unique.

Everyone who has used the platform for even a short time knows the following:

- You must have unit tests that cover at least 75% of your code in order to deploy your software to a production organization.
- You can deploy code directly from a development or sandbox organization to a production organization (using changesets, the IDE or ANT), or you can create a package (managed or unmanaged).

Those who have come to Apex programming from any other programming environment also know this:

- Debugging on the Force.com platform is shockingly primitive compared to most other modern development platforms.

For those who are religious about platforms, please don't take offense at the latter comment. Cloud software development is still a relatively new phenomenon, and does not lend itself to the same debugging techniques as other types of software development. That doesn't change the fact that even basic debugging concepts such as the ability to set breakpoints and watchpoints, and during them reset the current execution location, inspect and modify variables, or modify code, are completely lacking.

In the introduction to this book I emphasized that it is not a re-hash of the documentation and that I expect it to be used as a supplement, not a replacement, for the Force.com documentation. Keep this in mind as you read the next few chapters, as I will not elaborate (beyond a brief mention) on unit test strategies that are recommended in the documentation (but not always followed). I won't describe the Developer Console (which has improved con-siderably over time), and I won't walk you step by step through the packaging or deployment process.

Instead, you'll learn that there are actually many types of unit tests, and the design patterns you should use will depend both on the type of unit test, and on the way you plan to deploy the appli-cation.

You'll learn how you can build debugging features into your appli-cation to supplement the capabilities built in to the platform, and get around some of its limitations.

And you'll learn design patterns and best practices for deployment that vary by deployment type. In particular, you'll learn design patterns that are critical for deploying a reliable and maintainable managed package.

One more thing before we proceed.

You may have already noticed a common theme in the past few paragraphs, one that represents another way in which the Force.com platform is unique. There is a tendency for most devel-opers to write code first and then worry about deployment. Even where deployment is considered early in the design, it is rarely a major factor in the actual design and architecture of an applica-tion. But on the Force.com platform, the type of deployment you intend to do has a huge impact on design. Design patterns that represent best practices for a consultant building a custom solu-tion for a specific organization, are in some cases radically different from the design patterns that are best practices for a developer creating a managed package for the AppExchange. The chapters that follow will address both types of deployment, and how that choice will impact your design efforts.

9 – Debugging and Diagnostics

When it comes to testing, debugging and diagnostics, it's very tempting to start the conversation with unit tests. The fact that you have to develop unit tests to deploy Force.com applications almost demands that every Apex developer engages in test-driven development to some degree.

However, I'm going to hold off the in-depth discussion of unit test design patterns until the next chapter, even though you will inevitably use unit tests as part of your debugging efforts. It's important not to confuse goals with the means used to attain them, and unit tests are just one tool – a means to an end.

What really are your goals when dealing with debugging and diagnostics? And what is the difference between them?

Debugging is the process of figuring out why software is working incorrectly and fixing the problem. To debug software you really want to have the following:

- A way to reproduce the problem
- A way to capture data about the problem
- A way to modify the code to try different ways of solving the problem

Diagnostics generally refers to the second bullet - capturing data about the operation of the software. Let's look at the first two of these issues in the context of an Apex application.

Reproducing Problems

Your first step in debugging any problem is to find a way to reproduce it. Since debugging is an iterative process, you'll want to be able to reproduce it easily and quickly – you may need to reproduce it many times before you can fully resolve the issue.

During development, the easiest way to reproduce an error is using test classes. Remember that you can use the SeeAllData attribute on a test class to view or hide existing data in an organization. You can (and should) create "throwaway" test classes as needed to debug specific problems.

You can run anonymous Apex in the Developer Console. It is often faster to run an anonymous Apex script and view the results in the Developer Console than it is to edit and run a test class. This, along with its additional capabilities, makes it particularly useful for iterative debugging. Unlike test classes, anonymous Apex works on actual data – so you will probably want to delete any objects that you create during the test.

When it comes to debugging bulk code, don't forget to look beyond just unit tests. The various data import and bulk operations available using the Salesforce.com user interface can be useful, as can the Apex Dataloader. You can also use the API to set up or clear data, or even perform tests using languages such as Java, C# or VB .NET.

Sometimes, of course, you'll just have to do things by hand with the Salesforce.com user interface.

What if you can't reliably reproduce a problem? This can happen for a number of reasons:

- The issue is load dependent – you may be hitting timeouts that only occur when the Salesforce instance you are using is heavily loaded.
- The issue is sequence dependent – there are many situations on the Force.com platform where the order of results or operations is indeterminate. Examples include queries

without an Order By clause, the order of objects within a bulk operation, and the order of triggers.

- Synchronization issues when multiple threads (multiple users or asynchronous operations) are taking place.

In these cases, you may have to rely on diagnostics - capturing information about problems when they occur.

Diagnostic Data

If you are coming to Apex from another language, in particular a desktop environment such as Visual Studio or Eclipse, you may feel that when it comes to obtaining information about a running application you are taking a step back into the dark ages – the 1970's or 80's. Gone is the ability to set even simple breakpoints or watchpoints and, during them, view and modify variables, or reset the execution location and continue. As for the latest technologies for capturing execution history and being able to rewind to a previous state and continue execution – don't even think about it.

Apex code runs in a shared environment. You simply can't have one piece of code freeze a thread or lock the database. Perhaps someday Salesforce.com will provide developers with Salesforce instances inside of virtual machines where this might be possible, but in the meantime, your options are limited.

The primary source for capturing runtime data from Apex are the debug logs. The debug logs have the following characteristics:

- They are limited in size.
- You can control the level of detail of the data you are capturing at the class level. Capture enough detail and you can view the values of variables – but you are more likely to exceed the maximum log size.

- You can use the System.Debug statement to add debug data to the log. Those statements can be hard to find in large debug logs.

- The Developer Console has the ability to extract and organize data from the debug logs, but only if the debug logs don't exceed a certain size (that is smaller than the maximum debug log size).

- The platform stores only a limited number of debug logs.

- When instructed to capture debug logs, the monitoring continues for a limited time or number of logs. Continuous logging is possible for the current user using the Developer Console, though the number of logs kept is limited.

- Debug logs are generated for a particular running user.

- Debug logs do not capture detailed data from managed packages unless you are the package owner and log in via the Subscriber portal.

As a result of these characteristics, it's not unusual to find yourself in the following debug cycle:

- Reproduce the error to obtain a log file and find a problem.
- Add some debugging code.
- Override the detail level of one or more classes so as not to exceed the maximum debug log size.
- Repeat

Though sometimes frustratingly slow, this approach does work for debugging during development. But it borders on useless in other scenarios:

- Because debug log monitoring is time limited, they are not effective for monitoring the ongoing operation of an application. In other words, if you are trying to track down an intermittent exception, you cannot count on debug monitoring to capture the data you need.

- Debug logs are of limited use for debugging managed packages. In particular, when developing a managed package, the debug log excludes most debug information when running the managed package after deployment to a test system. And you must do this kind of testing because there are bugs that can appear in a managed package only after it is deployed due to the addition of the namespace prefix to objects and fields.

- Debug logs are useless for tracking down package installation errors – they simply aren't available at that time.

Instrumenting Apex - I

How important is the ability to monitor and capture diagnostic data on a deployed application?

That depends.

If you are a consultant building an organization specific solution, it can be hard to justify the added investment in diagnostic code, even though (as you will see), the investment can result in faster debugging.

If you are building a managed package for distribution, instrumentation is critical. Any investment in diagnostic code will pay for itself many times over in reduced support costs.

Our example will build on much of the code you've seen up until now. A single trigger, OnOpportunity3, will dispatch triggers to class DiagnosticsMain. This class is based on the concepts for central dispatching covered in Chapter 6. Two sets of functionality are implemented for this trigger: the functionality from Chapter 4 in which contact roles are processed during an opportunity stage change, and the functionality from Chapter 6 in which tasks are created during an opportunity probability change. I won't include all of the listings here because you have already seen them (the previous code is largely copied verbatim into the new sample classes). The example architecture is shown in Figure 9-1.

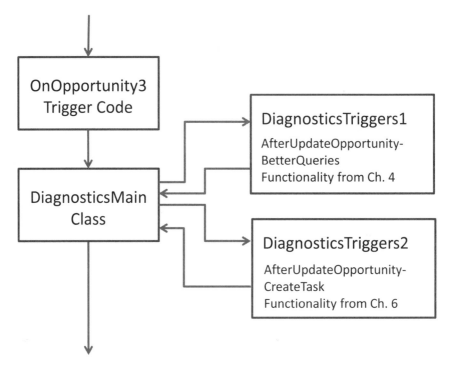

Figure 9-1 – Base example for instrumentation

The instrumentation is designed to capture information during an execution context. In addition to simple text debug information, it incorporates the ideas of levels – where each time you enter a function the level number increments, and each time you exit a function the level number decreases. This acts as a simple call stack.

The DiagnosticsInstrumentation class starts by defining some static variables along with the DiagnosticEntry class that contains the current level and description of a diagnostic entry.

```
public static Boolean DiagnosticsEnabled = true;

private static List<DiagnosticEntry> DiagnosticLog;
private static Integer CurrentLevel = 0;

private class DiagnosticEntry
{
    Integer level;
    String description;

    public DiagnosticEntry(string entrydescription)
    {
        level = CurrentLevel;
        description = entrydescription;
    }
}
```

The DiagnosticEnabled flag makes it possible to enable or disable the diagnostic system. This is important because the diagnostics code does use script lines, and in later implementations, performs SOQL and DML calls as well. So you'll want to be able to disable the diagnostics in cases where limits are an issue.

Four main diagnostic functions are defined as follows:

```
public static void Push(String functionname)
{
    Debug('Entering: ' + functionname);
    CurrentLevel+=1;
}

public static void Debug(String debugstring)
```

```
{
    if(!DiagnosticsEnabled) return;
    if(DiagnosticLog==null)
        DiagnosticLog = new List<DiagnosticEntry>();
    DiagnosticLog.add(new DiagnosticEntry(debugstring));
}

public static void Pop()
{
    if(CurrentLevel>0) CurrentLevel-=1;
    if(CurrentLevel==0)
        System.Debug(LoggingLevel.Info,
        'Diagnostic Log\n' + CurrentLog());
}

public static void PopAll()
{
    CurrentLevel=0;
    Pop();
}
```

The Push function should be called at the start of every function, and the Pop function on exit (though you may want to avoid putting them in small functions that are called frequently to avoid capturing too much data). The Pop function includes a test to make sure the level can't be decremented below zero – that prevents errors in cases where you forget to include a Pop statement for a function or one of its exit points.

PopAll is used for exception handling – you'll see why later.

Finally, there's a function to display the current diagnostics log:

```
public static String CurrentLog()
{
    if(DiagnosticLog == null) return null;
    String spaces = '                         ';
    String result = '';
    for(DiagnosticEntry de: DiagnosticLog)
    {
        Integer endindex = 3 * de.level;
        if(endindex >= spaces.length())
            endindex = spaces.length()-1;
        result += spaces.substring(0,endindex) +
            de.description + '\n';
    }
    return result;
}
```

In addition to adding the Push and Pop statements, in this example add a Debug call right before the Test.StartTest method in the TestDiagnostics1.cls unit test methods, and another one right after the MainEntry function (that is called by the triggers) that provides information about the trigger:

```
DiagnosticsInstrumentation.Push('MainEntry TriggerObject: ' +
TriggerObject + ' IsBefore: ' + IsBefore + ' IsInsert: ' +
IsInsert + ' IsUpdate: ' + IsUpdate);
```

After running the tests in the TestDiagnostics1 file, you can scroll up from the end of the file to find a debug statement that looks something like this:

```
10:07:59.228 (32228697000)|USER_DEBUG|[36]|INFO|Diagnostic Log
Entering: MainEntry TriggerObject: Opportunity IsBefore: true
IsInsert: true IsUpdate: false
Entering: MainEntry TriggerObject: Opportunity IsBefore: false
IsInsert: true IsUpdate: false
```

```
Entering: MainEntry TriggerObject: Opportunity IsBefore: true
IsInsert: true IsUpdate: false
Entering: MainEntry TriggerObject: Opportunity IsBefore: false
IsInsert: true IsUpdate: false
Starting testing: UpdateOpportunityTest
Entering: MainEntry TriggerObject: Opportunity IsBefore: true
IsInsert: false IsUpdate: true
Entering: MainEntry TriggerObject: Opportunity IsBefore: false
IsInsert: false IsUpdate: true
    Entering: DiagnosticsTriggers1.MainEntry
      Entering: DiagnosticsTriggers1.
              AfterUpdateOpportunityBetterQueries
    Entering: DiagnosticsTriggers2.MainEntry
      Entering: DiagnosticsTriggers2.
              AfterUpdateOpportunityCreateTasks2
```

So what have we accomplished here?

You now have the ability to quickly find, near the end of the diagnostic log, a complete snapshot of the execution tree of your application. You can embed additional debug statements anywhere you wish, and view them without the clutter that is embedded in the debug logs. You can build on this concept further. For example, you could add a timestamp to each diagnostic entry, and add a System.Debug statement to the diagnostic debug function to make it easy to cross reference entries in the diagnostic log to the corresponding statements in the debug log.

Having all of the key information you need in one place that is easy to find can speed up the debugging process by reducing the time it takes to understand what happened during each test iteration.

But that's not all.

Did you notice how the Debug statement in the Pop function included a diagnostic level of info:

```
System.Debug(LoggingLevel.Info,
'Diagnostic Log\n' + CurrentLog()
```

This allows the debug statement to appear in the debug log even when the filter is set to Info – which captures less data than the default 'Debug' level, and far less data than the 'Finest' level used by default in the Developer Console. You could even set this level to Warning or Error to allow the debug information to appear at those levels as well.

This allows you to capture diagnostic data for tests that normally exceed the maximum debug log size, since choosing the lower level of data capture reduces the debug log size.

Faster debugging and avoiding debug log size limits are both incredibly useful, but are only the beginning. To see why, we first need to look at yet another benefit of the central trigger dispatching architecture described in Chapter 6.

Centralized Exception Handling

Whether you are a consultant or creating a managed package, the one thing you don't want to have happen is for your end users to be working in Salesforce.com and suddenly see Figure 9-2 ....

Figure 9-2 – User experience for unhandled Apex exceptions

Yes, it's the dreaded Apex exception. The ultimate bad user experience. In this case, the exception was created in the
AfterUpdateOpportunityCreateTasks2 function using the following code:

```
List<Task> newtasks;
// Comment out this line to fake a runtime error
//newtasks = new List<Task>();
```

Of course, this is an artificial example, but it represents a realistic
scenario. Even with the best testing and QA, it is always possible
that one of these will slip by. This is especially true on the
Force.com platform because these kinds of errors can be created
well after deployment of your application by the later addition of a
required field, workflow or validation rule. Even the best developer can't anticipate every possible scenario that could cause an
Apex exception.

You could wrap every single line of code and every method in its
own exception handler. However, a centralized trigger dispatching
architecture lends itself perfectly to centralized exception handling.

First, add the following method to the DiagnosticsInstrumentation
class:

```
public static void DebugException(Exception ex)
{
    Debug('Exception occurred line ' +
    ex.getLineNumber() + ' - ' + ex.getMessage() +
    ' stack: ' + ex.getStackTraceString())
);
}
```

Now the DiagnosticsMain.MainEntry method is modified to trap all exceptions.

```
public static void MainEntry(String TriggerObject,
    Boolean IsBefore, Boolean IsDelete,
    Boolean IsAfter, Boolean IsInsert,
    Boolean IsUpdate, Boolean IsExecuting,
    List<SObject> newlist, Map<ID, SObject> newmap,
    List<SObject> oldlist, Map<ID,SObject> oldmap)
{
    DiagnosticsInstrumentation.Push('MainEntry
        TriggerObject: ' + TriggerObject + '
        IsBefore: ' + IsBefore + ' IsInsert: ' +
        IsInsert + ' IsUpdate: ' + IsUpdate);
    try
    {
        if(activefunction != null)
        {
            activefunction.InProgressEntry(
                TriggerObject, IsBefore, IsDelete,
                IsAfter, IsInsert, IsUpdate,
                IsExecuting, newlist, newmap, oldlist, oldmap);
            return;
        }

        if(TriggerObject == 'Opportunity' && IsAfter && IsUpdate)
        {
            activefunction = new DiagnosticsTriggers1();
            activefunction.MainEntry(TriggerObject,
                IsBefore, IsDelete, IsAfter, IsInsert,
                IsUpdate, IsExecuting,  newlist,
                newmap, oldlist, oldmap);
        }

        if(TriggerObject == 'Opportunity' && IsAfter && IsUpdate)
        {
            activefunction = new DiagnosticsTriggers2();
```

```
            activefunction.MainEntry(TriggerObject,
                IsBefore, IsDelete, IsAfter, IsInsert,
                IsUpdate, IsExecuting,  newlist,
                newmap, oldlist, oldmap);
        }
        DiagnosticsInstrumentation.Pop();
    }
    catch(Exception ex)
    {
        DiagnosticsInstrumentation.DebugException(ex);
        DiagnosticsInstrumentation.PopAll();
    }
}
```

Now, if you look at the debug logs that result from this exception, you will see the following (slightly reformatted here for the book):

```
09:43:22.798 (30798283000)|USER_DEBUG|[41]|INFO|Diagnostic Log
Entering: MainEntry TriggerObject: Opportunity IsBefore: true
IsInsert: true IsUpdate: false
Entering: MainEntry TriggerObject: Opportunity IsBefore: false
IsInsert: true IsUpdate: false
Entering: MainEntry TriggerObject: Opportunity IsBefore: true
IsInsert: true IsUpdate: false
Entering: MainEntry TriggerObject: Opportunity IsBefore: false
IsInsert: true IsUpdate: false
Starting testing: UpdateOpportunityTest
Entering: MainEntry TriggerObject: Opportunity IsBefore: true
IsInsert: false IsUpdate: true
Entering: MainEntry TriggerObject: Opportunity IsBefore: false
IsInsert: false IsUpdate: true
    Entering: DiagnosticsTriggers1.MainEntry
        Entering: DiagnosticsTriggers1.
            AfterUpdateOpportunityBetterQueries
    Entering: DiagnosticsTriggers2.MainEntry
        Entering: DiagnosticsTriggers2.
```

```
            AfterUpdateOpportunityCreateTasks2
            Exception occurred line 37 - Attempt to
            de-reference a null object stack:
Class.DiagnosticsTriggers2.
   AfterUpdateOpportunityCreateTasks2: line 37,
   column 1
Class.DiagnosticsTriggers2.MainEntry:
   line 7, column 1
Class.DiagnosticsMain.MainEntry: line 31,
   column 1
Trigger.OnOpportunity3: line 3, column 1
```

Of course, centralized exception handling isn't a replacement for exception handling in individual functions where you actually need to perform specific processing based on the exception. But it's a great way to make sure that users rarely experience Apex exceptions.

The risk of this approach is that you might fail to see errors that need to be addressed. Which brings us back to instrumentation, and to the real benefits of building a diagnostic system.

Instrumenting Apex – II

Displaying diagnostic data in the system debug log is fine when you're debugging, but because they only capture data for a specific user, and the number of debug logs that are stored is limited, debug logs are fairly useless for instrumentation.

The diagnostic system described here, on the other hand, is perfect for instrumentation. All you need is a place to store the data.

In this example, a custom object named "DebugInfo" that has a single long text custom field named "DebugData" is used to store the diagnostic information for Apex exceptions.

The DiagnosticsInstrumentation.DebugException method is modified as follows:

```
public static void DebugException(Exception ex)
{
    String exceptioninfo = 'Exception occurred line ' +
        ex.getLineNumber() + ' - ' + ex.getMessage()
        + ' stack: ' +
    ex.getStackTraceString();
    Debug(exceptioninfo);
    DebugInfo__c dbg = new DebugInfo__c(
        DebugData__c = CurrentLog());
    if(DiagnosticsEnabled) insert dbg;
}
```

Now, when a user performs an operation that previously displayed the Apex error message, the operation will succeed (the centralized exception handler traps and ignores the error). A new DebugInfo record will be created with information about the exception as shown in Figure 9-3.

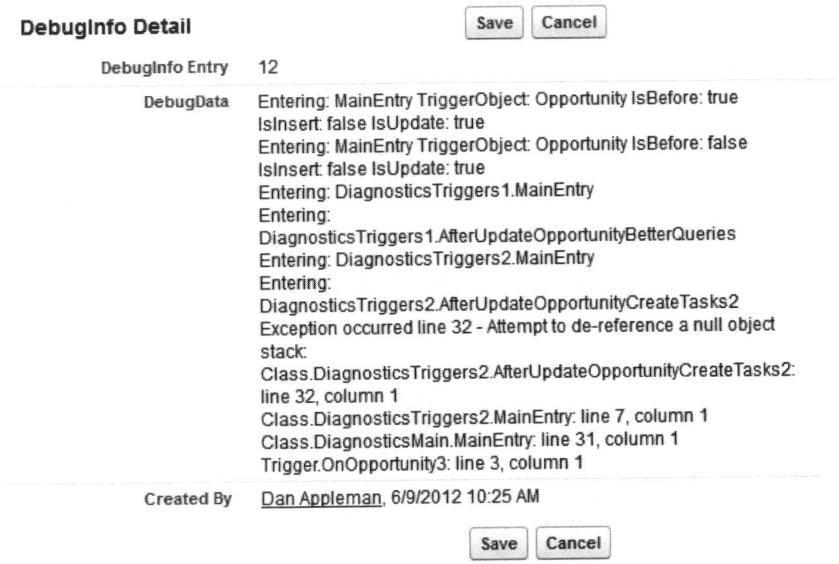

DebugInfo Detail Save Cancel

DebugInfo Entry 12

DebugData Entering: MainEntry TriggerObject: Opportunity IsBefore: true
IsInsert: false IsUpdate: true
Entering: MainEntry TriggerObject: Opportunity IsBefore: false
IsInsert: false IsUpdate: true
Entering: DiagnosticsTriggers1.MainEntry
Entering:
DiagnosticsTriggers1.AfterUpdateOpportunityBetterQueries
Entering: DiagnosticsTriggers2.MainEntry
Entering:
DiagnosticsTriggers2.AfterUpdateOpportunityCreateTasks2
Exception occurred line 32 - Attempt to de-reference a null object
stack:
Class.DiagnosticsTriggers2.AfterUpdateOpportunityCreateTasks2:
line 32, column 1
Class.DiagnosticsTriggers2.MainEntry: line 7, column 1
Class.DiagnosticsMain.MainEntry: line 31, column 1
Trigger.OnOpportunity3: line 3, column 1

Created By Dan Appleman, 6/9/2012 10:25 AM

Save Cancel

Figure 9-3 – DebugInfo objects hold diagnostic information

Let's take a moment and review what we have accomplished.

- You now have the ability to monitor your application for Apex errors 24x7 (as compared to debug logs that are only active when enabled).

- All users are monitored (as compared to debug logs that monitor a single user).

- You can capture and store large amounts of diagnostic data (as compared to debug logs where the number of logs stored is limited).

- You can effectively capture stack trace information even with managed packages (where the detailed stack trace information is hidden unless you are logged into a system via the subscriber system of the license management app). On those systems the final stack trace in the debug entry will be missing, but you'll still have the stack trace information generated via the Push and Pop methods of the DiagnosticsInstrumentation class.

But that's not all.

The instrumentation system shown here is extremely simple. There are other features you may want to implement:

- Set up a scheduled Apex operation that periodically Emails to a support Email address all of the DebugInfo records that occurred during that period. In many cases, this can allow you to be proactive and address client or customer problems before they are even aware they exist. Note – you probably don't want to send an Email on each error that occurs so as to avoid exceeding Email limits.

- Instead of just storing text string, consider capturing the data in XML. This not only allows you to capture more (or at least more structured) data, it makes it possible to perform automated processing of debug information, both on the deployed system and when handling incoming debug Emails.

- You can extend this concept to work with VisualForce controllers, as long as you're careful to only save diagnostic records at times when DML operations are allowed.

- Remember to periodically delete old diagnostic data to avoid data bloat. This should be automated as well, perhaps during a scheduled Apex method where you delete all entries older than a specified period, or you can simply limit the number of records stored.

Thinking about Debugging and Diagnostics

Debugging, diagnostics and instrumentation are closely related. While most debugging occurs (or should occur) during development, in reality it is not unusual to need to debug systems after deployment. This is particularly true with Force.com due to the enormous variability of organizations, and because the development system (be it a developer or sandbox) is never 100% identical to the production system. Even a full sandbox rarely has all of the production system apps enabled and fully functional. Even the best unit tests can't reproduce every scenario, especially in organizations with large amounts of data.

Building your own diagnostic infrastructure is a valuable supplement to the monitoring capabilities built into Force.com. It can provide critical information for debugging applications on production systems and in cases where unit tests are limited. It can provide ongoing monitoring to improve your ability to support your clients and customers.

For those of you creating managed packages, the value in building some kind of diagnostics and instrumentation system is clear and compelling.

The case is more difficult for consultants. In many organizations, Apex code is developed on an as-needed and ad-hoc basis. While any one trigger or class may be designed and coded properly, there is often no overriding architecture. It is difficult to justify building a diagnostics system for that "one simple trigger". It's only after that one simple trigger evolves into a dozen "simple" triggers that you begin to wish someone had built in and enforced instrumentation from the beginning.

However, all is not lost. Sooner or later most companies reach a point where, due to growth or changes in business process, they need to revisit their implementation and make substantial changes. That's a perfect time to review all of the existing code and invest in diagnostic infrastructure that will pay off in the long term.

10 – Unit Tests

Why Johnny Won't Test

The following is from the Apex language documentation.

Salesforce.com recommends that you write tests for the following:

Single action

Test to verify that a single record produces the correct, expected result.

Bulk actions

Any Apex code, whether a trigger, a class or an extension, may be invoked for 1 to 200 records. You must test not only the single record case, but the bulk cases as well.

Positive behavior

Test to verify that the expected behavior occurs through every expected permutation, that is, that the user filled out everything correctly and did not go past the limits.

Negative behavior

There are likely limits to your applications, such as not being able to add a future date, not being able to specify a negative amount, and so on. You must test for the negative case and verify that the error messages are correctly produced as well as for the positive, within the limits cases.

Restricted user

Test whether a user with restricted access to the sObjects used in your code sees the expected behavior. That is, whether they can run the code or receive error messages.

Doesn't that sound wonderful?

But how often do developers actually follow those recommendations? Very rarely – and then only for the most trivial examples.

In fact, the only consistent testing practice that I've seen is the development of unit tests needed to meet the 75% code coverage requirement for deployment.

Does this mean that most Apex developers are lazy and incompetent? Not at all.

The language documentation recommendations are great in principle, but are actually somewhat simplistic – and they don't reflect the real world priorities of developers.

Let's start by considering why most developers don't follow all of these recommendations.

Time and Money

Employees are often under enormous time pressure. Force.com developers are expensive, and most organizations are understaffed. Sometimes this results in code being written by beginners who don't really know how to write good test code. Sometimes developers just have so much to do that it's more important to meet a deadline or add a feature than add additional unit tests to code that seems to work correctly (and quite possibly does work correctly). Afterwards, it's hard to justify going back to build more test code.

Consultants face pressure both on bidding and on execution. Test code is expensive. It's not unusual for the amount of test code in an Apex application to exceed the amount of functional code, which some might interpret as doubling the cost of development. If a consultant's bid includes all of the recommended test code, they might lose the contract to someone who doesn't – the client probably will not know the difference. During implementation, whether the job was bid hourly or flat rate, any test code beyond the minimum potentially eats into profits, as even hourly consultants rarely have an open-ended budget. Test code that exceeds the original estimate requires a consultant to either go back for more money (which makes the consultant look bad and less likely to be trusted in the future), or absorb the cost.

Product developers, as you will see, have the most to gain from unit tests. But they too suffer pressure to meet release deadlines, and are also often understaffed.

As you can see, the pressure to cut corners on testing is enormous.

Perfect Testing Doesn't Exist

Programming today is a race between software engineers striving to build bigger and better idiot-proof programs, and the Universe trying to produce bigger and better idiots. So far, the Universe is winning. – Rick Cook

Testing for all positive and negative cases sounds good, but it's actually quite difficult (and in many cases theoretically impossible). This is especially true for the negative cases, where users have an infinite capability to come up with input that you never imagined.

Apex Applications Can be Complex

As the Force.com platform has evolved, the platform limits have gradually been relaxed. This is in part due to customer demand, and in part because advances in hardware infrastructure makes it possible to support greater developer limits.

As those limits have been relaxed, the potential complexity of Apex applications has grown. In a complex application, it becomes increasingly difficult and costly (and eventually impossible) to test every code permutation. Moreover, testing individual units of code does not guarantee operation of the application as a whole – you need a completely different set of tests to validate functionality of the integrated system.

So while the Salesforce.com recommendations can work well for trivial code, more and more code on the platform is non-trivial.

Testing in the Real World

At this point it would be easy to say "I know testing is expensive and difficult, but you should do it anyway because…"

A. You are a software professional.

B. Salesforce.com says you should.

C. I say so.

Speaking as a software professional, these are all rather silly reasons. Test code is no different from any other code – you write it because it is cost effective to do so.

If we're really going to address the issue of testing beyond the required 75% code coverage, we need to start with the economic justification for those tests – because at some point, somebody has to pay for them.

So forget (for the moment) the recommendations from the Salesfore.com documentation, and let's view the problem from a completely different direction.

What are unit tests intended to accomplish?

As it turns out, we write tests for many different purposes. And each of those purposes can have a completely different cost justification, and require completely different design patterns.

Here are the most common reasons (in no particular order) for writing test code on the Force.com platform:

- Meet the Salesforce.com 75% code coverage requirement.
- Validate the functionality of code (does it meet requirements or specifications).
- Bulk testing – can the code handle bulk operations?
- Debugging – reproducing errors during the development process.
- Regression testing – does a change you are making break existing code?
- Compatibility with target systems – will the application work on a production system after it is deployed?
- Configuration validation – is an organization configured correctly for the application?

Viewed this way, testing takes on a whole new level of complexity. Let's take a quick look at each of these in turn, after which we'll examine how they impact testing best practices.

Code Coverage

This is the one type of test that every Apex developer must build. It is also the last type of test you should write. Focus on implementing the other tests first. Then go back and add test code as needed to meet and maximize code coverage.

While ideally every test you write will use Assert statements to validate functionality, there is a temptation to leave out validation when trying to meet code coverage requirements. It's alright to do so for trivial cases – for example, when writing tests for Visual-Force pages there may be cases where you will write code that reads property values in order to achieve code coverage on property Get statements, and completely ignores the resulting values.

If you are creating a managed package, be sure to add at least one Assert statement to each test class, even if it is as simple as System.Assert(true). Failing to do so will generate warnings in the Force.com security source scanner that you may have to explain during security review.

Validating Functionality

This is perhaps the most important reason to write unit tests. Every project starts with a set of requirements. If you're lucky, they may even be written down somewhere. At some point, you have to validate if your code performs as specified.

You should always write test code to validate functionality. Even if you didn't have to write test code to meet code coverage requirements, it would still be worthwhile, as the cost of writing functional test code is more than offset by reduced debugging and QA costs.

Unit tests make it relatively easy to place an organization into a known state. And changes to the database made during unit tests are not persisted. This makes functional validation in unit tests dramatically faster than manual testing.

If you focus on functional testing, you'll often find that this is sufficient to meet code coverage requirements.

Bulk Testing

Bulk testing is an aspect of validating functionality. Though listed here separately, as you will see, unit test best practices dictate that all of your tests be written as bulk tests, even when running the test for single objects.

Debugging

Don't hesitate to write "throwaway" tests to help resolve bugs or to verify your understanding of Apex behavior. Just be careful to actually throw away tests that don't follow best practices (you'll read more about unit test best practices later in this chapter).

Regression Testing

Regression testing refers to the practice of verifying that changes in your code don't break existing functionality. On the Force.com platform, regression testing takes on a greater significance, in that it is also used to verify that changes in the configuration of an organization don't cause errors in your application.

This latter factor makes automation of regression tests more critical than it is in other environments. Unlike other platforms, where you would normally perform regression testing only after making changes to your application, and can often limit your testing to those areas of the application impacted by changes, under Force.com it is advisable to perform regression testing after any changes to an organization. That includes everything from installation of new applications, to creation of workflows, validation rules or required fields.

The good news is that the unit tests you create to validate functionality are the same ones you will use for regression testing. The knowledge that they will be used for regression testing as well only serves to emphasize the importance of those tests, and to justify the investment needed to go beyond the minimal requirements to achieve code coverage.

Compatibility with Target Systems

This aspect of unit testing applies mostly to packages, as compatibility testing of an application written on a sandbox for a specific organization is inherent in the functional testing.

Not only do your unit tests have to meet the 75% code coverage requirement during deployment, as of API version 23 the tests have to pass as well. Before that, it was possible to ignore test errors during installation.

Aside from the code coverage requirement, installation unit tests are essential for validating that your application will run correctly on a target system – as you may not even have access to the system for manual testing.

Writing unit tests for deployment is a complex topic that will be covered later in this chapter.

Configuration Validation

Unit tests can be used to verify that an application or organization has been configured correctly after installation. These tests can be created using the oninstall=false option so that they do not run during installation.

A good example of this kind of test is verifying that a user has configured lead field mapping of custom fields. You can't perform this test during installation, as it is not possible to configure lead field mapping during the installation itself – it has to be done manually after installation. But you can create unit tests to run after installation that validate that the manual lead field mapping configuration was done correctly.

Revisiting Recommendations

Looking at testing based on the goals described in the previous section makes it easier to develop a realistic test strategy.

Consultants working on a single organization should focus on validating functionality (both positive and negative tests), bulk testing and debugging.

Developers working on managed packages should invest more on the breadth of functional tests to enable the best possible regression testing as well. They are also more concerned with target compatibility and configuration validation.

Common Test Design Patterns

Now that you have a clear picture of the many roles that unit tests play, let's take a look at how those roles influence best practices in unit test development.

Centralize Object Initialization

It is very common to create test objects in a unit test. It is always advisable, where possible, to test functionality against objects that you create rather than relying on existing objects in an organization. In fact, the default setting for the SeeAllData attribute on unit tests is false, meaning that unit tests by default can't even access most existing data in an organization.

You should never create objects in the test function itself. You should, instead, create a single static method for creating each type of test object. For example, a typical function for creating opportunity objects would be as follows:

```
public static List<Opportunity>
    CreateOpportunities(String basename, Integer count)
    {
        List<Opportunity> results =
            new List<Opportunity>();
        for(Integer x = 0; x< count; x++)
        {
            results.add(new Opportunity(Name = basename
                    + String.valueOf(x) ));
        }

        return results;

    }
```

An alternate version of this function can create an opportunity and at the same time initialize any default field values:

```
public static List<Opportunity>
    CreateOpportunities(String basename, Integer count)
{
    List<Opportunity> results = new List<Opportunity>();
    for(Integer x = 0; x< count; x++)
    {
        Opportunity op =
            (Opportunity)Opportunity.sObjectType.newSObject(
                                        null, true);
        op.Name = basename + String.valueOf(x);
        results.add(op);
    }
    return results;

}
```

This latter approach does have a cost in terms of CPU time, but can make your code more robust when it comes to handling validation rules and workflows on a target system. You'll soon see another approach for initializing default field values that is particularly useful for managed packages.

The unit test uses the initialization function as follows:

```
newopportunities = CreateOpportunities('optest_',
                            NumberOfOpportunities);
for(Opportunity op: newopportunities)
{
    op.CloseDate = Date.Today().addDays(5);
    op.StageName = 'Prospecting';
}
insert newopportunities
```

All of the test code in your application should share the same object initialization functions that set default field values that you specify. Your code should then modify any additional values as needed before actually inserting the object.

Centralizing initialization has no immediate benefit, but reduces the lifecycle costs of your application. That's because it is very possible that at some point in the future, someone will add a required field or validation rule to the object that will cause the object creation to fail during the test. If you centralize object creation, you will be able to add the required field to the initialization function, thus resolving the problem for all associated tests with a single edit, instead of having to track down every place in your code where that object is created, make the change and deploy the update.

This is particularly important for developers of managed packages, as it simplifies use of pre-deployment settings – a technique you'll read about later in this chapter.

Organizing Tests into Classes

One of the dilemmas you will inevitably face is deciding how many test methods to include in a test class.

The nice thing about including multiple test methods in a class is that it helps organize test methods and makes it easier for them to share common code. You've already seen how the sample code implements the UpdateOpportunityTest test method using a call to InitTestObjects to initialize test objects, and another call to ValidateOCRs to validate the results. The test method itself mainly defines the parameters of the test. Clearly, it would be very easy to leverage the InitTestObjects and ValidateOCRs function to implement multiple tests using very little additional code.

The disadvantages of including multiple test methods in a class are twofold:

- You can't run individual tests in a class. This slows down the execution of the test class – leading to frustrating delays during debugging.
- All of the test methods in a test class share the same debug log. Using multiple test methods in a class increases the chances that you will exceed the maximum debug log size. The test you are interested may not even appear in the debug log.

There is no ideal solution to this problem. My own approach is to combine related tests into a test class and comment out or disable those that I'm not interested in during debugging (later in this chapter you'll learn how to disable individual tests without commenting them out).

Keep in mind that having common code that is shared by test methods is not a strong reason for including multiple test methods in a test class. You can always place common code into a regular class, or into a public test class. Use a public test class if the common code is used only for tests. Use a regular class if the common code can also be used by your application.

Use Bulk Test Patterns

You may recall that in Chapter 4, I recommended that all of your code be built using bulk patterns. This applies to test code as well.

To understand why this is particularly important for unit tests, consider the reason for doing bulk testing in the first place. It is almost entirely related to validating functionality. It has little to do with code coverage or other testing goals.

If your bulk tests are a separate set of tests, you incur high costs for little added benefit. Not only is there the cost of building the tests, and running a second set of tests, but there is also a performance hit during deployment - bulk tests tend to run more slowly than single record tests.

Given the high cost and performance cost involved in creating a distinct set of bulk tests, along with the fact that they rarely add any code coverage over single object tests, there's a strong temptation to skip them, and in many cases that's exactly what happens.

However, if you write every unit test as a bulk test, the story changes. The incremental cost of writing a bulk test instead of a single object test is negligible – especially if you have focused on learning those patterns from the start.

You can use a static constant to define the number of objects to use during the test as shown here:

```
private static final Integer
    NumberOfStageUpdateOpportunities = 5;

static testMethod void TestTaskCount() {
    List<Opportunity> ops = CreateOpportunities('optest_',
        NumberOfStageUpdateOpportunities);
```

While debugging, use an object count of one or two. This will provide excellent performance. Using an object count of two will also validate your bulk handling in terms of functionality (though not against limits).

To perform bulk testing against limits, just increase the value of the object count constant.

The key thing to realize here is that you don't need to do bulk tests all the time. You do need to validate bulk handling during development, but you can often avoid bulk tests during deployment to speed the deployment process. If you are building on a sandbox for a specific organization, passing bulk tests on the sandbox virtually guarantees that the bulk processing will work on the production organization. The same applies if you are deploying an AppExchange managed app, which has its own set of governor limits.

If you are deploying an unmanaged application, or one that is not an AppExchange managed app, it is more important to test bulk handling on the target system. But that doesn't mean you need to do the testing during deployment. What you should do in that case is replace the object count constant with a field from a custom setting.

During deployment, when the custom setting is not yet defined, use a default object count of one or two to achieve a rapid deployment. After installation, set the custom setting value to a high number (typically 200), and use Apex test execution to validate that the application runs correctly.

If you build every unit test as a bulk test, and make the batch size configurable, you gain all of the benefits of bulk testing at almost no cost, making this a clear best practice for all Apex test development.

Other Limit Testing and SeeAllData

Bulk tests serve two purposes – they validate the functionality of your batch handling, and they ensure that you can perform your processing within the governor limits.

But bulk tests alone are not always sufficient to guarantee that your code will not exceed limits. There are a number of reasons for this:

- Test setup in unit tests also has governor limits, meaning there is a limit to the number of objects that you can insert into the database for testing.
- Triggers and web service calls are not the only sources of batch data. Queries and searches may return large numbers of records that can be difficult to process within limits. In fact, they can return larger numbers of records than you can generally create during your unit test setup.

The problems you will run into tend to fall into three categories:

- Queries or searches that have too broad a criteria, where the number of records returned exceeds limits.
- Queries or searches that return a large number of records, where the processing of the records causes you to exceed script limits.

- Queries that are not selective, and thus cannot be processed successfully on systems with very large numbers of records.

The best way to avoid these problems is through careful design. But as careful as you may be, it's always possible to miss something, so it's always a good idea to test as well. But these tests require large amounts of data that cannot be created during the test itself.

In the past, you would often catch these issues early because test code had access to all of an organization's data. In fact, test code queries would have to be written very carefully to filter out existing data so that your tests were only looking at objects created during the test.

The SeeAllData test attribute defaults to false, which hides most of an organization's data from a test. This can simplify test code and speed test execution, but it also prevents a unit test from finding the kinds of limit errors that can happen on large organizations.

For this reason, it is actually better to set SeeAllData to true for tests on code that performs queries or searches on objects other than those that are part of a trigger or API batch (including related objects). Even if you use criteria in your query to view only those records created during the test, the fact that there are a large number of records on the system will help expose any non-selective queries that may exceed limits.

Even setting the SeeAllData attribute to true is not sufficient to fully test an application against limits. Ultimately it requires testing on a large organization. A common approach is to set up a developer organization or enterprise sandbox specifically for these tests and use the Apex dataloader to import large amounts of data, and then perform manual testing of the application. A more sophisticated approach involves writing an external application, typically in Java or .NET, that uses the API to populate data, perform operations, and validate the results – essentially building an external "unit test" that, through the use of multiple API calls, bypasses the limits of regular unit tests.

However, the cost of these kinds of tests on large organizations can usually only be justified by developers of managed packages. If you are developing a managed package for distribution, you absolutely need to perform those tests. If you are a consultant working on an individual organization, just be aware that these kinds of problems can occur. If possible, test your code on a full sandbox. If you only have a configuration sandbox available, allow extra time for launch and testing in case problems turn up during deployment.

Testing Exception Handlers

Good programming practice calls for generous use of exception handlers in your code, even for cases where you believe an exception is unlikely or even impossible. One of the unintended consequences of the 75% code coverage requirement is that it tends to discourage use of exception handlers because they are difficult to test, and the lack of those tests counts against the code coverage requirements.

The secret to testing exception handlers is actually quite simple: use a static variable to generate a fake exception.

Here's an example from the DiagnosticsMain class:

```
public static ITriggerEntry activefunction = null;

public static Boolean FakeException = false;

public static void MainEntry(String TriggerObject,
    Boolean IsBefore, Boolean IsDelete, Boolean
    IsAfter, Boolean IsInsert, Boolean IsUpdate,
```

```
Boolean IsExecuting, List<SObject> newlist,
Map<ID, SObject> newmap, List<SObject> oldlist,
Map<ID,SObject> oldmap)
{
    try
    {
        if(fakeexception && activefunction==null )
            activefunction.InProgressEntry(
            TriggerObject, IsBefore, IsDelete, IsAfter,
            IsInsert, IsUpdate, IsExecuting, newlist,
            newmap, oldlist, oldmap);
        .
        .
        .
    }
    catch(Exception ex)
    {
        DiagnosticsInstrumentation.
            DebugException(ex);
        DiagnosticsInstrumentation.PopAll();
    }
}
```

This will result in a null reference exception the first time the code is invoked (and every time thereafter in this particular case).

The test code is as follows:

```
static testmethod void TestFakeException()
{
    DiagnosticsMain.FakeException = true;
    List<Opportunity> ops = CreateOpportunities('optest_',
        NumberOfStageUpdateOpportunities);

    for(Opportunity op: ops)
    {
        op.CloseDate = Date.Today().addDays(5);
```

```
    op.StageName = 'Prospecting' ;
}
Test.StartTest();
insert ops;
Test.StopTest();
}
```

Now this presents a rather interesting question. This unit test does give you code coverage for the exception, and it also executes the DiagnosticsInstrumentation DebugException and PopAll methods.

Should you add an assert statement to validate functionality at this point? Or is it just enough to test the code coverage and perhaps add a dummy assert statement so as not to raise a flag with the Force.com security source scanner?

If you have other code to test the DiagnosticsInstrumentation class, you can probably get by without an assert here. Otherwise, you could add some code to verify that an exception actually occurred.

```
List<DebugInfo__c> dbg = [Select ID from DebugInfo__c];
system.Assert(dbg.size()>0);
```

This particular test takes advantage of the fact that SeeAllData is false by default. That means that when the test runs, there are no DebugInfo__c objects visible to the test code. Any that are found after the test were created during the test.

You can also test exception blocks by defining and throwing your own exception type as follows:

```
class IsTestingException extends Exception{}

if(system.Test.isRunningTest() && FakeException)
{
    IsTestingException e = new IsTestingException();
    throw e;
}
```

Testing and Static Variables

The previous example demonstrates a technique that actually has many applications. Just as static variables are a powerful tool for controlling execution of an application, they are a powerful tool for controlling testing. Some circumstances where you can also use them include:

- Testing exception handlers.
- Initializing data within Apex triggers that cannot be initialized before the start of a test. For example: When creating an opportunity from a contact page, Salesforce.com creates the OpportunityContactRole for the opportunity before the Opportunity After-Insert trigger. You can't reproduce this in a test class. But you can use a static variable in your After-Insert trigger to cause your application to add an OpportunityContactRole object before continuing with your regular trigger code. This allows you to accurately test this scenario. You can use the @TestVisible attribute to ensure that only test code can access the specified static variable.
- Modifying query criteria. This is typically done when using the SeeAllData = true option to restrict queries to data you have created, or to limit the size of a query for a batch Apex test to ensure that only a single batch execution call takes place. In either case, you can use a static variable to select

from two static SOQL queries, or to add a filter term to the WHERE clause of a dynamic SOQL query.

Testing, Configuration and Custom Settings

It is very common for applications to use custom settings to store configuration information. This poses two challenges for test code:

- It is essential that your test code work correctly if no custom setting objects are defined (as is the case with initial deployment).

- It is essential that your test code not be dependent on the values of custom settings. Otherwise, test code can start failing as users modify application settings. This is especially painful with regards to package upgrades.

The easy way to address this is with the SeeAllData attribute set to false. You can then create new custom setting objects as needed for the tests. However, as you saw earlier, there are cases where you will need to have SeeAllData set to true. In those cases it is essential that you never use existing custom setting values unless you are certain that they can't impact your test.

There is a subtle problem that can occur if your test code inserts, updates or deletes custom setting objects. As test code can run asynchronously, when more than one test tries to update a custom setting object, you can see intermittent record locking errors.

The solution is to use a centralized custom setting design pattern as shown in the AppConfigSupport class in the sample application. This class provides access to the AppConfig__c custom setting that contains the EnableDiagnostics__c field.

```
public class AppConfigSupport {

    private static AppConfig__c testconfig = null;

    public static AppConfig__c GetAppConfig()
    {
        if(Test.isRunningTest() && testconfig!=null)
            return testconfig;

        AppConfig__c theobject =
            AppConfig__c.getInstance('default');
        if(theobject==null || Test.isRunningTest())
        {
            theobject = new AppConfig__c();
            theobject.name = 'default';
            theobject.EnableDiagnostics__c =
                (Test.isRunningTest())? true: false;
            if(!Test.isRunningTest()) Database.Insert(theobject);
            else testconfig = theobject;
        }
        return theobject;
    }

    public static Boolean DiagnosticsEnabled
    {
        get
        {
            return GetAppConfig().EnableDiagnostics__c;
        }
    }

}
```

It's always a good idea to centralize access to custom settings as shown here. Use individual properties to access fields for easy readability and to provide flexibility to add additional functionality in the future.

The testconfig static variable holds a copy of the object to use during testing. When running tests, a new instance of the object is always created and initialized to the default values. Default values can vary depending on whether you are in a test or regular context.

There is some argument in favor of refactoring the code for a clearer separation of the code that runs in a test context versus a regular context, instead of using multiple Test.isRunningTest() conditions as shown here. Though more cluttered and less efficient, the code shown here does centralize the object initialization, which can be an advantage on custom settings with many fields. But it's more of a stylistic choice than a question of best practices.

The key issue is that the GetAppConfig() object does not insert or update the custom setting object during a test. Test code can easily modify object values by calling GetAppConfig() and setting the field directly. Alternatively, you can add set methods to the class to set individual fields on the custom setting.

Testing and Fragile Code

Another problem that can occur with both custom settings and organization data has to do with interactions with existing code that relies on those settings or data being present. This is illustrated in figure 10-1:

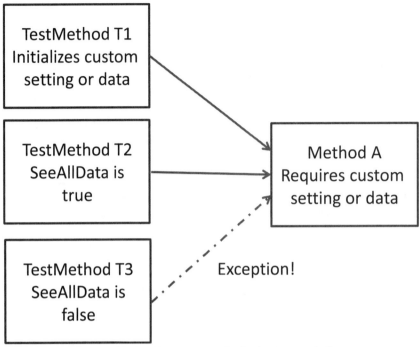

Figure 10-1 – Base example for instrumentation

Let's say that method A is written to assume that organization data is present, and will raise an exception if it is missing. There are two ways that test methods can handle this situation. They can initialize the data as part of the test initialization. Or they can be defined with the SeeAllData=True attribute. Any test with SeeAllData=False that does not initialize the necessary data will fail.

This is easy enough to deal with inside of an organization, but what if TestMethod T3 is part of a managed package? Managed packages cannot access custom settings that are not part of the package, and are restricted on the types of organization data that they can access.

This leaves developers of managed packages with three options:

- Insist that customers fix their existing code so that it will fail gracefully (without exceptions) if data is missing (good luck that).

- Use SeeAllData=True on any test that has the potential to run organization code.

- Implement a mechanism to turn off tests (you'll see how this is done shortly).

It goes without saying that all code should be written to fail gracefully when custom settings or data is missing. But the reality is that a great many Apex developers still write their code assuming custom settings will be initialized and data present – either they don't realize that this is an issue, or they are focused on doing what is easy and cheap to implement in the short term.

The OnInstall Attribute

You can use the OnInstall attribute to specify if test code should run during a deployment or upgrade. This attribute poses an interesting dilemma:

- It makes it easier to get a package installed on a system, in particular if one or two test classes are particularly troublesome.

- It shifts detection and possibly debugging of problems from install time to after a package is deployed. This can reduce the number of package iterations you have to go through to resolve a problem.

Generally speaking, you should not use this as a way to get around tests that aren't passing during install. There is value it detecting problems early. In fact, there are only a limited number of cases where you should consider setting this attribute to false:

- If you do have distinct bulk tests and single object tests, set OnInstall false on the bulk tests.

- You have a test designed to validate application configuration – configuration information that is only present after deployment. This kind also requires that the SeeAllData attribute be set to true, as it will typically directly access the custom setting objects (unlike normal tests, you don't want to bring the configuration to a known state before running this kind of test).

The following is an illustration of the first case, where the single object version of the test is run on deployment, but the bulk version is not.

```
@istest(oninstall=true seealldata=false)
static void CreateTaskTestSingle()
{
    CreateTaskTest(1);
}


@istest(oninstall=false seealldata=false)
static void CreateTaskTestBulk()
{
    CreateTaskTest(100);
}


static void CreateTaskTest(Integer
        NumberOfOpportunities)
{
    List<Opportunity> ops = CreateOpportunities('optest_',
        NumberOfOpportunities);
        .
        .
```

What about tests that are just problematic – that are failing on installation, often with minimal or cryptic error messages? In those cases, you may want to just get the package deployed so you can research the problem further. If you are a consultant working on deployment to a single organization, setting OnInstall to false may be a good approach.

But if you are developing a managed package, there is a better way as you will soon see.

Testing in Managed Packages

When it comes to testing, managed packages pose unique challenges:

- Instead of targeting a single organization, your unit tests, like the rest of your code, have to take into account the virtually infinite possibilities of organization configuration and metadata – at least as much as is possible.
- Managed packages protect your intellectual property by hiding your Apex code and other details relating to the operation of your application. This includes hiding stack trace information that can be crucial for debugging.
- Because of the high cost of supporting multiple versions of an application, your tests need to be able to adapt to a particular organization while still maintaining a single code base.

Let's start by addressing the second point – finding a way to capture better debug data during a package installation.

Roll Your Own Stack Trace

In Chapter 9 you saw how centralized exception handling could trap and report on an exception deep within your code. When viewed in the debug log on a development system or unmanaged package, you could see the following detailed entry:

```
AfterUpdateOpportunityCreateTasks2
        Exception occurred line 37 - Attempt to
          de-reference a null object stack:
Class.DiagnosticsTriggers2.AfterUpdateOpportunityCreateTasks2:
    line 37, column 1
Class.DiagnosticsTriggers2.MainEntry: line 7, column 1
Class.DiagnosticsMain.MainEntry: line 31, column 1
Trigger.OnOpportunity3: line 3, column 1
```

When installing a managed package, the same simulated error results in the following report:

```
Problem:

1. Apex Classes(01pU0000000xsYM) testdiagnos-
tics2.TestTaskCount()
System.AssertException: Assertion Failed: Expected: 5, Actual: 0
(AdvancedApx1)
```

That "(AdvancedApx1)" at the end is the namespace, which is all the information available – Salesforce.com will not display the stack trace for a managed package. All we know from this is that an assert failed in the TestTaskCount method.

It's true that centralized exception handling is hiding the actual exception from the report, but even if the exception was visible, all you would see is the type of exception and the line number. The method in which the exception occurred is also hidden.

Fortunately, the assert statements all have the option to include additional debugging information. This, combined with a simple extension to the existing diagnostic code, makes it possible to implement a basic stack trace.

It starts by adding two static variables to the DiagnosticsInstrumentation class:

```
private static List<String> stacktrace = new List<String>();
public static string ExceptionTrace = '';
```

The stacktrace list serves as a stack. The ExceptionTrace string will
hold the debug information for the most recent exception recorded
using the DebugException method.

The Push and Pop methods implement the stack. Note that they
are always active – they don't depend on the DiagnosticsEnabled
setting.

```
public static void Push(String functionname)
{
    Debug('Entering: ' + functionname);
    CurrentLevel+=1;
    Stacktrace.add(functionname);
}

public static void Pop()
{
    if(CurrentLevel>0) CurrentLevel-=1;
    if(CurrentLevel==0)
        System.Debug(LoggingLevel.Info,
        'Diagnostic Log\n' + CurrentLog());
    if(StackTrace.size()>0)
        StackTrace.remove(StackTrace.size()-1);
    }
```

The DebugException method stores detailed information about
the exception including the contents of the stacktrace list into the
ExceptionTrace variable. It does not use the getStackTrace method
of the Exception object because that method does not return a

stack trace when used in a managed package (unless you are logged into an organization via the subscriber portal of the License Management Application).

```
public static void DebugException(Exception ex)
{
    String exceptioninfo = 'Exception occurred line '
        + ex.getLineNumber() + ' - ' + ex.getMessage()
        + ' stack: ' + ex.getStackTraceString();
    Debug(exceptioninfo);
    DebugInfo__c dbg = new DebugInfo__c(DebugData__c =
        CurrentLog());
    ExceptionTrace = ' Exception occurred line ' +
        ex.getLineNumber() + ' - ' + ex.getMessage();
    for(String st: stacktrace) ExceptionTrace += ' | ' + st;
    ExceptionTrace += ' |\n ';
    if(DiagnosticsEnabled) insert dbg;
}
```

Now change the assert in the TestTaskCount test method from:

```
System.AssertEquals(NumberOfStageUpdateOpportunities,
    tasks.size());
```

to:

```
System.AssertEquals(NumberOfStageUpdateOpportunities,
    tasks.size(),'Error in TestTaskCount. Stacktrace:
    ' + DiagnosticsInstrumentation.ExceptionTrace);
```

When you try to install the package now, you'll see the following report:

Problem:

```
1. Apex Classes(01pU0000000xsaI)
testdiagnostics2.TestTaskCount()
System.AssertException: Assertion Failed: Error in
TestTaskCount. Stacktrace:  Exception occurred line 32 - Attempt
to de-reference a null object | MainEntry TriggerObject:
Opportunity IsBefore: false IsInsert: false IsUpdate: true |
DiagnosticsTriggers2.MainEntry |
DiagnosticsTriggers2.AfterUpdateOpportunityCreateTasks2 |
 : Expected: 5, Actual: 0
(AdvancedApx1)
```

The additional information provided by this report can save hours of debugging time.

You should always include descriptive information of some kind in each assert used in a managed package, if only to distinguish between multiple assert statements. Implementing a more robust reporting mechanism such as this one is also well worth the investment.

Disabling Tests for Install

If you have experience deploying packages, you may have found one thing suspicious about the previous example. It uses a simulated exception that always occurs. But Salesforce.com runs all tests in a package before the package can be uploaded. How is it possible that I could upload a package that has a test failure so that it would fail on deployment?

The answer relates to the previous challenge – how does one adapt an application to a specific organization (in this case disabling an individual test) without modifying the underlying code. Because that is exactly how this was done – the TestTaskCount test method was disabled on the development organization so that the package could be uploaded. The test was then active during deployment, where it failed.

While you can do a lot to make a test flexible, there is currently no way to dynamically figure out which custom fields have validation rules that would prevent you from creating test objects. And there is no way to disable individual tests that are failing on a target organization during install because of a legitimate system configuration such as a workflow.

Obviously, you need a way to get information onto the target system that can be used to control the behavior, or even bypass, your unit tests. You can't use a custom object - because they aren't present on the system until the package is installed. You can't really use an existing custom setting or custom object, even using dynamic SOQL, because your tests that have the SeeAllData attribute false won't see that data and you couldn't read an organization's custom setting anyway.

What you really need is some kind of metadata resource that can be predeployed onto a system before package installation, that can be read by test code to modify its behavior for that system. And you need this resource to be visible to your test code regardless of the value of the SeeAllData attribute.

Fortunately, there is exactly that kind of resource available – a static resource.

For this example, we'll define a static resource named Apx1Predeployment. The resource will consist of a simple text file where each line is in the form:

```
disable:n
```

where n is the number of a test to disable.

The function IsTestDisabled takes a test number as a parameter, then loads the static resource and determines if that test number appears on any of the disable commands.

```
public static Boolean IsTestDisabled(Integer testnumber)
    {
    List<StaticResource> resources = [Select Body from
        StaticResource where Name = 'Apx1Predeployment' ];
    if(resources.size()==0) return false;
    String contents = resources[0].Body.ToString();
    if(contents==null) return false;
    List<String> lines = contents.split('\\n');
    for(String line:lines)
    {
        List<String> entries = line.split(':');
        system.debug('entries ' + entries);
        try
        {
            if(entries[0]=='disable' &&
                Integer.valueOf(entries[1].trim())==
                testnumber) return true;
        }
        catch(Exception ex){}
    }
    return false;
}
```

This implementation ignores errors in the file format. It is a simple implementation – you could make it more efficient using regular expressions, but the point here is to illustrate the approach.

The TestTaskCount method calls IsTestDisabled to determine if it should run as follows:

```
static testMethod void TestTaskCount() {
      if(IsTestDisabled(1)) return;
```

You can assign a test number to every test method, or share a test number among several related test methods. This approach allows you to effectively shut down individual tests on any target system by first uploading a static resource containing the list of tests to disable.

This idea can be extended further:

- Static resources can be deployed via the API – so you can actually automate the process of disabling individual tests for an organization.
- Instead of using a text file, consider using an XML file. This can allow you to store more complex deployment information.

Object Initialization Revisited

A similar approach can be used to deal with the problem of validation rules on a target system that prevent your test code from creating test objects.

In our example, this is demonstrated through a validation rule named "Enforce Tracking Number" that has the following error condition:

```
ISBLANK(TrackingNumber__c )
```

Installing on a system where the validation rule is active results in the following error message:

```
System.DmlException: Insert failed. First exception on row 0;
first error: FIELD_CUSTOM_VALIDATION_EXCEPTION, Tracking number
must be set for opportunities: []
(AdvancedApx1)
```

The nice thing about this error is that the installation report actually provides useful information. The challenge is, what to do with it?

The answer is to extend the static resource approach to allow the setting of additional field values on objects. In this example, the information is specified by a line in the format:

```
objecttype:fieldname=value
```

To set the Tracking Number field on opportunity, the entry could be:

```
Opportunity:TrackingNumber__c=somevalue
```

The SetDefaultFields function handles field initialization as follows:

```
public static Boolean SetDefaultFields(String objecttype,
List<SObject> theobjects)
    {
    List<StaticResource> resources = [Select Body from
        StaticResource where Name = 'Apx1Predeployment' ];
    if(resources.size()==0) return false;
    String contents = resources[0].Body.ToString();
    if(contents==null) return false;
    List<String> lines = contents.split('\\n');
    for(String line:lines)
    {
        List<String> entries = line.split(':');
```

```
try
{
    if(entries[0]==objecttype)
    {
        List<String> fieldinfo = entries[1].split('=');
        for(SObject obj: theobjects)
        {
        obj.put(fieldinfo[0], fieldinfo[1]);
            // Implemented only for strings
        }
    }
}
catch(Exception ex){}
}
return false;
}
```

This implementation is designed to handle any object type and batches of records, making it an efficient solution.

The problem with this implementation is that it will only work with strings. A more robust approach would query describe information to obtain the correct data type, and perform the necessary conversions. This is left as an exercise to the reader.

As with the IsTestDisabled code, it ignores exceptions. At a minimum, you would probably want to add a system.debug statement within the exception handler to help diagnose problems.

Here is where the benefit of centralized object initialization really pays off. Instead of having to call SetDefaultFields throughout your test code, all you need to do is modify the CreateOpportunities function to the following:

```
public static List<Opportunity> CreateOpportunities(String
basename, Integer count)
{
    List<Opportunity> results = new List<Opportunity>();
    for(Integer x = 0; x< count; x++)
    {
        results.add(new Opportunity(Name = basename +
            String.valueOf(x) ));
    }
    SetDefaultFields('Opportunity', results);
    return results;
}
```

You can, of course, combine this approach with using the sObjectType.newSObject method that can initialize default object values.

This solution is not a perfect one. Validation rules can be complex, and it's possible that there is no one value that will work to allow your test code to create objects. In that case, you would have to disable that validation rule or make a code change to proceed with the install. Still, this approach will work in a great many cases.

11 – Designing for Packages

Whether you are a computer scientist or an experienced software developer, you tend to build a mental framework of how certain things are usually done. Part of the fun of learning a new language or platform are the surprises that you run into along the way – the innovations or unexpected decisions of the language or platform authors that challenge your preconceptions.

Sometimes those surprises don't make any sense at first. More than one Apex developer I know was puzzled initially by the unusual approach that Force.com takes with static variables. Yet, after becoming familiar with the framework, it becomes obvious that the Force.com creators knew what they were doing, and it's hard to imagine static variables working any other way.

Like most Apex developers, I started out doing consulting work on specific organizations. It was only when I started designing my first managed package that I ran into what was, for me, the greatest surprise of all. I came to realize that in many cases the best practices for developing a package are completely different from the best practices when developing for a single organization.

I've been both consulting, and writing production commercial code on other platforms, for a long time. There is always a difference between the two – turning specialized code into production code is always a big effort. But aside from the obvious need to generalize functionality, that effort usually consists of polish – improved exception handling, instrumentation, and support code or application metadata.

This was the first case I recall where writing code for a redistributable package called for completely different design patterns.

You already saw this in the last chapter. The ability to disable tests, or dynamically initialize field values, has absolutely no value when you are deploying organization specific code from a sandbox to a production organization. There is little need to add additional debugging information to asserts, when installation reports include unobfuscated stack trace information.

Many, if not most of the design patterns that you've already learned in this book, are heavily influenced by packaging best practices that turn out to also be advantageous for organization specific code. In this chapter you'll not only learn a number of common (or useful but uncommon) approaches to use when developing Force.com packages, you'll also see a number of other cases where the best practices for packaging should actually be avoided when developing code for single organizations.

Dynamic SOQL and Dynamic Apex

Dynamic SOQL allows you to use Apex code to define a SOQL query string at runtime. Static SOQL is hard-coded and validated at compile time.

If you are building an application for a specific organization, you should almost always use static SOQL for two reasons:

- Compile time validation reduces the chance of runtime errors and speeds the debugging process, as all syntax and most semantic errors are caught during compilation.
- Static SOQL is not vulnerable to SOQL injection attacks, where a user provided parameter can change the meaning of the query to expose more data than intended.

In fact, it's rare that you'll ever need to use dynamic SOQL when building code for a single organization, as most user specified criteria can be incorporated into a query using variables. In cases where query terms vary depending on user input, you can often use conditional code to select among several static queries rather than building a dynamic query.

For managed applications, the exact opposite is the case – dynamic SOQL is often preferred over static SOQL. There are three reasons for this:

- Your application may need to reference fields that do not necessarily exist on target systems.

- Your application may need to adapt to features that may or may not be available on target systems.

- Using dynamic SOQL, you can use a central list of fields to query for specific objects across multiple queries. If you add a new field to a later version of the application, you can add it in one location instead of editing multiple queries. In complex applications, this reduces the chance that you will fail to query for a required field.

Let's look at the first two of these in detail.

Organization Dependent Fields

Let's say your application has some functionality in which processing is influenced by the RecordType of an object. When writing code for a single organization, you wouldn't think twice about querying the code like this:

```
List<Lead> rtypes = [Select ID, RecordTypeID from Lead Limit 1];
```

In a managed package, this approach is deadly. That's because this code will fail to install on any organization that does not have record types defined for leads. You see, on the Force.com platform, if no record type is defined for an object, the RecordTypeID field doesn't even exist – so any query that tries to use it will fail.

The correct way to use record types in a managed package is as follows:

```
Boolean LeadHasRecordType =
    Schema.Sobjecttype.Lead.Fields.getMap().containskey(
        'recordtypeid');

String fieldstring = 'ID ';
if(LeadHasRecordType) fieldstring += ', RecordTypeID ';
List<Lead> rtypes = Database.Query('Select ' +
    fieldstring + ' from Lead Limit 1');
```

First use Apex describe functionality to find out if the desired field (in this case RecordTypeID) exists on the object. If so, add it to the query string. This is a very simple illustration of course. In a larger application, you would use caching to avoid multiple tests to determine if a particular field exists.

There are numerous other objects and fields where this situation arises, enough so that it is a rare application where using dynamic SOQL in this manner is unnecessary.

It is important to note that this code presents no risk of SOQL injection – all of the data used in the query is generated programmatically.

Organization Dependent Features

When you upload a package, Salesforce.com calculates a set of requirements for the target system. Figure 11-1 shows the package requirements for the sample code up until this point.

Package Requirements	
Notify installers of any requirements and incompatibilities with this package. The requirements selected below will be displayed to the administrator prior to download.	
ⓘ Administrators will not be allowed to install this package if their salesforce.com configuration does not meet the requirements specified (some requirements have been automatically detected as part of the sharing process).	
Feature	**Required**
New Opportunity Save Behavior	☑
Workflow	✓
Additional Feature Requirements	**Required**
Account Team	☐

Figure 11-1 – Sample package requirements

So far the only requirements relate to opportunities (which is the main object used in the examples), and workflow – and that only because the sample workflow used earlier to demonstrate errors is currently part of the application.

Let's say you add a feature to your application that can optionally display information about the products related to an opportunity. At some point you might have a query on the Product2 object, of which the following is a trivial example:

```
List<Product2> aproduct = [Select ID from Product2 Limit 1];
```

One side effect of this code is that you've now added a package dependency. If you upload the package now, you'll see the requirements specified in Figure 11-2.

Package Requirements

Notify installers of any requirements and incompatibilities with this package. The requirements selected below will be displayed to the administrator prior to download.

> ⓘ Administrators will not be allowed to install this package if their salesforce.com configuration does not meet the requirements specified (some requirements have been automatically detected as part of the sharing process).

Feature	Required
New Opportunity Save Behavior	☑
Product	✓
Workflow	✓

Additional Feature Requirements	Required
Account Team	☐

Figure 11-2 – Package requirements now has Product2

Every time you add a requirement to your package, you potentially reduce the number of systems on which your package can install, and thus the number of potential customers.

For large functional components, it might make sense to use a base package and create an extension package to support this kind of flexibility – where the extension package has its own, more restrictive, set of requirements.

But for optional features – where your application adapts to the existing configuration of the system, dynamic SOQL allows you to avoid adding requirements to your package. Because the Apex compiler is not aware that you are using a feature, it won't impose that feature as a requirement.

Remember though, that you must check if a feature is available on a target system before using it, or implement good exception handling – as any attempt to access an object or field that is not present on the system will result in an exception. This includes test code.

Dynamic SOQL and Security Reviews

Use of dynamic SOQL is one of the red flags checked for during the AppExchange security review. You should include in your submission an explanation that you are using dynamic SOQL in order to allow your application to process fields that may or may not exist on a target system, and that the queries are generated programmatically and are not dependent on user input (assuming, of course, that this is accurate). Also note that you are taking SOQL injection precautions including escaping strings (the escapeSingleQuotes string method) on user input, and are validating any user specified field names if those apply to your application. Most of the security reviewers understand the tradeoffs involved, and will not raise this as an issue once they are confident that you are using dynamic SOQL correctly, and for the right reasons.

Dynamic Apex

Dynamic Apex refers to the ability to set and retrieve the values of object fields by specifying the name of the field at runtime.

Here is an example that combines dynamic SOQL and dynamic Apex to solve a common problem: how do you support currency conversion when multiple currency support is only available on some organizations?

In this example, the GetCurrencyConversionMap function returns a map of conversion values for each ISO code, where the value can be used to convert a specified currency to the current corporate currency (this differs from using the convertCurrency SOQL option that converts values to the user's currency).

The CachedCurrencyConversionMap map holds the cached value of the conversion map. The CorporateCurrency property can be used to retrieve the corporate currency (note the call to GetCurrencyConversionMap to make sure the backing property m_CorporateCurrency is set.

```
private static Map<String,double>
    CachedCurrencyConversionMap = null;

private static string m_CorporateCurrency = null;

public static string CorporateCurrency {
    get {
        GetCurrencyConversionMap();
        return CorporateCurrency;
    }
}
```

The GetCurrencyConversionMap function has to address the fact that the CurrencyType object does not exist on single currency organizations. All access to the object and its fields must be dynamic for the code to compile on a single currency organization.

```
public static Map<String, double>
    GetCurrencyConversionMap()
{
    if(CachedCurrencyConversionMap!=null)
        return CachedCurrencyConversionMap;

    Boolean CurrencyTestMode = false;
    if(Test.isRunningTest() &&
        !userinfo.isMultiCurrencyOrganization())
        CurrencyTestMode = true;
    if(!userinfo.isMultiCurrencyOrganization() &&
        !CurrencyTestMode) return null;
    List <SObject> ctypes = null;
    if(!CurrencyTestMode) ctypes  = database.query(
        'Select conversionrate, isocode,
        iscorporate from currencytype');
```

```
Map<String, double> isomap = new Map<String, double>();
if(!CurrencyTestMode)
{
    for(SObject ct: ctypes)
    {
        string ctcode = string.ValueOf(ct.get('isocode'));
        if(Boolean.valueof(ct.get('iscorporate')))
        {
            m_CorporateCurrency = ctcode;
        }
        double conversionrate = double.valueOf(
            ct.get('conversionrate'));
        if(conversionrate!=0)
            isomap.put(ctcode, 1/conversionrate);
    }
}
CachedCurrencyConversionMap =
    (CurrencyTestMode)? null: isomap;
return CachedCurrencyConversionMap;
}
```

The CurrencyTestMode variable is used to obtain at least some code coverage over the function on single currency organizations.

This example raises an interesting question. If your application uses currency conversion, should you enable multiple-currency support on your developer organizations?

The advantage of doing so is:

- You can actually test currency conversion on the developer organization.

The disadvantages of doing so are:

- It becomes easier to miss cases where dynamic SOQL and Apex are required. You'll catch those errors during testing instead of at compile time.
- You must make sure to test on single currency organizations.
- It takes longer to spin up new developer orgs because you have to put in a request to enable multiple currencies for each org.

It's usually better to keep your development orgs at the minimum feature set that you are targeting, and enable additional features on your QA organizations (which include both other developer orgs and sandboxes).

There are a variety of algorithms that benefit from dynamic Apex that are not related to packaging. As far as packaging design patterns go, the issues that apply to dynamic SOQL are the same ones that apply to dynamic Apex – you should always use dynamic Apex to access fields or objects that may not be present on a target system, and to avoid fields that, if referenced, impose an undesired requirement for package installation.

Person Accounts

If you create an application that references contacts, you need to be aware of a curious entity called a "person account". Person accounts only exist on organizations for which they are specifically enabled. They are not enabled by default, and in order to enable them you have to file a case, and convince Salesforce.com support that you really know what you are doing and that you understand that the conversion can't be reversed. Once the person accounts feature is enabled on an organization, it can never be disabled.

A person account is differentiated from a regular account by the account record type. Person accounts have the following characteristics with regards to Apex programming:

- Each person account has a "shadow" contact object. The ID of that object can be retrieved using the PersonContactID field on the account object.

- You can access standard contact fields for person accounts two ways – by querying the underlying contact and accessing the field as you would a normal contact field, or by accessing the field on the account using a special name that typically consists of the contact field name preceded by the word "Person". Thus, the contact Email field can be retrieved on the account using the field name PersonEmail. The contact fields FirstName, LastName and Salutation do not have this prefix.

- You can access custom contact fields for the person account object two ways – by querying the underlying contact and accessing the field as you would a normal contact field, or by accessing the field on the account using a special name that consists of the contact field name ending with the suffix __pc instead of __c.

- Contact triggers do not fire on person accounts. Only account triggers fire on these accounts, even if you change a field on the underlying Contact object.

If the package you are developing does not reference the contact object, you can probably ignore person accounts. Otherwise, you should design your code with them in mind, as packages that use contacts probably won't work correctly with person accounts without additional work.

Your first step in supporting person accounts will be to create a separate developer org and request that it have person accounts enabled.

Next, you can implement a couple of helpful functions to work with person accounts. The first is a static function to let your application determine if it is running on an organization with person accounts enabled.

```
private static Set<string> AccountFields = null;

public static Boolean IsPersonAccountOrg()
{
    if(AccountFields==null) AccountFields =
        Schema.Sobjecttype.Account.fields.getMap().keyset();
    return AccountFields.contains('personcontactid');
}
```

The IsPersonAccountOrg caches the set of account fields so that you can efficiently verify person account fields.

Another function that can prove useful maps contact field names to their equivalent person account name:

```
// Map from contact field to account field
public static String getPersonAccountAlias(String fieldname)
{
    fieldname = fieldname.ToLowerCase();
    // Case insensitive

    // Unchanged - FirstName, LastName, etc.
    if(AccountFields.contains(fieldname)) return fieldname;

    // Replace aliased __c with __pc
    fieldname = fieldname.replace('__c', '__pc');
    if(AccountFields.contains(fieldname)) return fieldname;

    if(AccountFields.contains('person' + fieldname))
        return ('person' + fieldname);
    return null;
```

```
}
```

You should always access person account fields using dynamic Apex, and should only access them on account objects where the PersonAccountID field is true.

Person Account Triggers

To see the challenges you can face when working with person accounts, consider the following very simple example – a Contact trigger that sets the Level__c field based on the LeadSource field as described in the following pseudocode:

```
If the LeadSource is 'Web' or 'Phone Inquiry', set Level__c to
'Primary'
Otherwise set Level__c to 'Secondary'.
```

If you were not concerned about person accounts, you would probably implement this as follows[3]:

```
trigger OnContact1 on Contact (before update, before insert)
{
    PersonAccountSupport.processContactTrigger1(
        trigger.isBefore, trigger.new, trigger.oldmap);
}
```

and in a class (in this case class PersonAccountSupport):

```
public static void processContactTrigger1(Boolean
```

---

[3] This particular sample code is located in class PersonAccountSupport because it is related to this section of the book. Despite the name of the class, the sample code at this point only applies to contacts.

```
    isBefore, List<Contact> newlist, Map<ID, Contact> oldmap)
{

    for(Contact ct: newlist)
    {

        if(ct.LeadSource=='Web' ||
            ct.LeadSource=='Phone Inquiry')
            ct.Level__c = 'Primary';
            else ct.Level__c = 'Secondary';

    }
}
```

The test code for this class might be as follows (see class TestPersonAccount in the sample code):

```
static testMethod void TestWithContacts() {
    List<Contact> contacts =
        TestDiagnostics2.CreateContacts('patst', 3);
    contacts[0].LeadSource='Web';
    contacts[1].LeadSource='Phone Inquiry';
    contacts[2].LeadSource='Other';
    Test.StartTest();
    insert contacts;
    Test.StopTest();
        // Seealldata is false, so we'll get the same
        // 3 contacts
    Map<ID, Contact> contactmap = new Map<ID,
        Contact>([Select ID, Level__c from Contact
        Limit 3]);
        system.assertEquals(contactmap.get(
            contacts[0].id).Level__c,'Primary');
        system.assertEquals(contactmap.get(
            contacts[1].id).Level__c,'Primary');
        system.assertEquals(contactmap.get(
            contacts[2].id).Level__c,'Secondary');
    }
```

How do we extend this to support a person account organization? There are a number of challenges:

- Not every account on a person account organization is, in fact, a person account. They are distinguished by record type.
- When creating or updating a person account, only the account trigger fires.

Your first thought might be to use a before trigger and to update the fields on the person account. For testing purposes we'll use an account trigger that processes both before and after triggers, though we'll only look at the before functionality for the moment.

```
trigger OnAccount1Trigger on Account (after insert,
    after update, before insert, before update)
{
    PersonAccountSupport.processAccountTrigger1(
    trigger.isBefore, trigger.new, trigger.oldmap);
}
```

Let's look at how the processAccountTrigger handles the before trigger case.

```
public static void processAccountTrigger1(Boolean isBefore,
    List<Account> newlist, Map<ID, Account> oldmap)
{
    if(!IsPersonAccountOrg()) return;

    if(isBefore)
    {
        // Using before approach
        String leadsourcealias =
            getPersonAccountAlias('LeadSource');
        String levelalias = getPersonAccountAlias('Level__c');
```

```
for(Account act: newlist)
{
    if(leadsourcealias!=null &&
    levelalias!=null &&
    act.get('PersonContactID')!=null)
    {   // Will only be valid on person
        // accounts
        if(act.get(leadsourcealias)=='Web' ||
            act.get(leadsourcealias)==
            'Phone Inquiry')
                act.put(levelalias,'Primary');
                else
                act.put(levelalias,'Secondary');
    }
  }
}
}
```

This approach suffers from two problems. First, it duplicates the functionality in the processContactTrigger1 code. That means that you have to support and maintain the same exact functionality in two different places, taking care to update both if any changes are required.

That may not mean much on a simple example like this, but for a complex example, this type of support or maintenance can result in significant costs over the lifetime of the software.

The second problem is more serious. Remember – this is a package, and your development and deployment organizations will almost certainly not be person account organizations. That means your code must meet code coverage requirements on a non-person account organization in order to be uploaded as a package.

Figure 11-3 illustrates the current architecture.

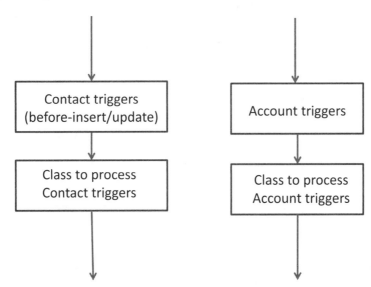

Figure 11-3 – Separate person account code is hard to maintain and test

The first problem is quite easy to solve, and demonstrates yet another reason why you should always implement your trigger code in a class.

Remember that every person account has a shadow contact object. Why not update that object directly?

You can't do this during a before trigger, but you can do it during an after trigger. The approach is as follows:

- Use an after-insert/update trigger on the Account object.
- If it is a person account organization, build a list of any accounts that have a PersonContactID value (these are the person accounts).
- Query for these contacts.
- Call the class method used to process contact triggers.

- Update the contacts (being careful not to process the re-sulting account trigger).

This approach is illustrated in Figure 11-4.

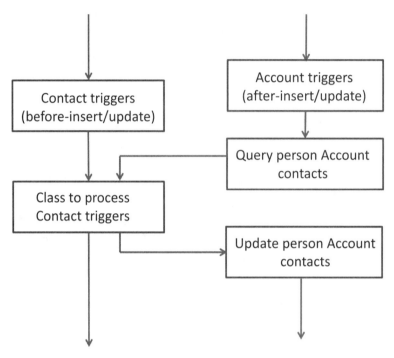

Figure 11-4 – Leveraging contact functionality when using person accounts

The way to address the code coverage issue is to use static varia-bles to allow most of your code to run even on a non-person account organization.

Here's what the resulting processAccountTrigger1 function looks like with both of these solutions implemented. Note that both the Before and After code is shown in the sample code – in practice you would only implement one of these approaches.

```
@TestVisible public static Boolean
    FakePersonAccountDuringTest = false;

public static List<ID> FakePersonContactIDs = null;

private static Boolean UpdatingPersonContact = false;

public static void processAccountTrigger1(Boolean isBefore,
    List<Account> newlist, Map<ID, Account> oldmap)
{
    if(!IsPersonAccountOrg() && !FakePersonAccountDuringTest ||
        UpdatingPersonContact) return;

    if(isBefore)
    {
        // Using before approach
        String leadsourcealias =
            getPersonAccountAlias('LeadSource');
        String levelalias = getPersonAccountAlias('Level__c');
        for(Account act: newlist)
        {
            if(leadsourcealias!=null && levelalias!=null
                && (!FakePersonAccountDuringTest &&
                act.get('PersonContactID')!=null))
            {   // Will only be valid on person accounts
                if(act.get(leadsourcealias)=='Web' ||
                act.get(leadsourcealias)=='Phone Inquiry')
                    act.put(levelalias,'Primary'); else
                    act.put(levelalias,'Secondary');
            }
        }
    }
    else
    {   // Better approach can work on after trigger
        Set<ID> personcontactids = new Set<ID>();
        for(Integer x = 0; x<newlist.size(); x++)
        {
```

```
        if(FakePersonAccountDuringTest ||
            newlist[x].get('PersonContactID')!=null )
            personcontactids.add(
            (FakePersonAccountDuringTest)?
            FakePersonContactIDs[x]:
            (ID)newlist[x].get('PersonContactID') );
    }
    if(personcontactids.size()==0) return;
    Map<ID, Contact> personcontacts = new Map<ID,
        Contact>([Select ID, LeadSource, Level__c
        from Contact where ID in :personcontactids]);
    ProcessContactTrigger1(true,
        personcontacts.values(), personcontacts);
    UpdatingPersonContact = true;
    update personcontacts.values();
    UpdatingPersonContact = false;
    }
}
```

There are a number of subtle issues to note in this code. First, the
FakePersonAccountDuringTest constant is tested before the check
for the PersonContactID field. Apex processes conditionals in left
to right order, so testing FakePersonAccountDuringTest first prevents the test for the PersonContactID field (which would cause a
missing field error) when testing.

Remember to gate the entire function with code that validates that
you are even running on a person account org, and exit if not (except when testing). Never forget that non-person accounts will
also raise this trigger.

The UpdatePersonContact flag is used to prevent the function
from being processed again when it is retriggered by the update to
the underlying Contact object. If you were using the centralized
trigger model described in Chapter 6, you wouldn't need to do this

– as the resulting trigger would be dispatched to the InProgressEntry method of the currently executing class instead of the MainEntry method – thus would be ignored by default.

The PersonContactIds set is used by the test code to provide fake shadow contacts in order to obtain code coverage.

To conclude, let's look at the test code:

```
static testMethod void TestWithAccounts() {
    List<Contact> contacts =
    TestDiagnostics2.CreateContacts('patst', 3);
    List<Account> accounts =
    TestDiagnostics2.CreateAccounts('patest', 3);
    contacts[0].LeadSource='Web';
    contacts[1].LeadSource='Phone Inquiry';
    contacts[2].LeadSource='Other';
    PersonAccountSupport.FakePersonContactIDs = new List<ID>();
    PersonAccountSupport.FakePersonAccountDuringTest = true;
    insert contacts;
    for(Contact ct: contacts)
        PersonAccountSupport. FakePersonContactIDs.add(ct.id);
    Test.StartTest();
    insert accounts;
    Test.StopTest();
    // Seealldata is false, so we'll get the
    //same 3 contacts
    Map<ID, Contact> contactmap = new Map<ID, Contact>
        ([Select ID, Level__c from Contact Limit 3]);
    system.assertEquals(contactmap.get(contacts[0].id).Level__c,
        'Primary');
    system.assertEquals(contactmap.get(contacts[1].id).Level__c,
        'Primary');
    system.assertEquals(contactmap.get(contacts[2].id).Level__c,
        'Secondary');
}
```

You might realize that this is not particularly good test code. In fact, it doesn't really test the person account logic at all – the Level__c fields are set during the insertion of the fake shadow contacts.

So what is the value of the test?

First off, try running the test with the FakePersonAccountDuringTest variable set to False, and look at the code coverage. You'll see about 37% on the PersonAccountSupport class. This increases to about 94% when the FakePersonAccountDuringTest flag is set true. In other words, this sample meets the primary requirement – illustrating how you can create tests that achieve code coverage of person account code on a non-person account organization.

Can you extend this to implement a true functional test? Sure you can. You'll need to query the RecordType object to find the person account record types. Then create accounts using that record type. Then create a test that uses dynamic Apex to validate the functionality. In doing so you've essentially recreated the same problem you had earlier – creating two distinct sets of code to perform the same function, one for contacts, and the other for person accounts.

However, if you use the second approach shown here - using the after triggers on the account to query the contacts and then call the same code that processes contact triggers, there really is no need to validate the overall functionality of the code in the person account tests. It is tested adequately by the contact trigger test code.

So all you need to do is validate the code that queries for shadow contacts and calls the contact trigger code. Because this code is very simple, you can probably get by with validating it manually as long as your unit test code provides adequate code coverage. It may not be a perfect solution – but it's a very good solution and is inexpensive to implement.

Other Best Practices

There are a number of other best practices to consider when developing a managed package.

Configuration

Managed packages are generally configured using custom settings. Decide which custom settings will be protected and which will be public when you create the custom settings. Visibility cannot be changed once a custom setting has been created..

Protected custom settings cannot be directly edited on the target organization (contents are hidden). That means that all of your settings will have to be configured through VisualForce pages. Though this can be a significant investment, it does have the advantage that all of the settings records and values are under your control – you don't have to worry about a system administrator manually changing and corrupting your settings. This, in turn, reduces the need for extensive error checking on custom setting data values.

On/off switch

Your application should have an "on/off" switch – a configuration setting that globally enables or disables your application. When your application is disabled all triggers should return immediately and most other functionality should be disabled. The only code that should work is your configuration code.

There are a number of reasons for doing this:

- It allows you to configure your application completely before making it active on a client system.
- In case of errors in the organization, it allows you to easily disable your application so that you can quickly determine

if it is your application that is causing the problem, or prove that it is not.

Avoid External ID and Rollup summary Fields on Standard Objects

There is an organization limit of no more than three external ID fields and ten rollup summary fields on an object. If you include these fields, and installing your application would cause these this limits to be exceeded, your application will fail to install. So it's best to avoid these field types if possible.

If you do use an external ID field, be sure to mark it as unique before you release your managed package. Once your package is released it is no longer possible to add the unique attribute. Records that have a non-unique external ID fields can only be upserted by system administrators – a restriction that you do not want to impose through your package.

Use a Single Code Base

You will almost inevitably run into a situation where you will want to implement some functionality in your application that is unique to a specific customer, and that cannot be implemented outside of the application through workflows or other Apex code.

This is easy enough to do using configuration once an application is installed, but you may also need to define unique behavior during installation.

For both of these cases, keep in mind the approach described in Chapter 10 for disabling individual tests and setting the initial values of object fields during tests by using information stored in static resources. This approach can easily be extended for other configuration purposes.

Doing so allows you virtually infinite flexibility within a single code base. This is important because the cost of supporting multiple code bases can be substantial.

Managing Organizations

You're going to accumulate developer organizations and sandbox organizations as time goes on. Don't try to do everything on a single org. Here are some of the organizations you will have, and some tips on using them.

- Code development org – This is the organization where each developer builds and tests code that they are working on. Most developers use the IDE for development, though the Developer Console is reaching the point of being reasonable for smaller projects. Keep in mind that you can have multiple projects in an IDE workspace. You may want one for development, and a separate project that defines metadata to deploy.

- Package test org – This is an org that will contain the full source code and both an unmanaged and managed package that uses a test namespace. You'll use this for package testing outside of the main package versioning. In particular, it will help you resolve problems with code that doesn't work correctly with a namespace assigned, and it will allow you to deploy an unmanaged package to get code quickly onto another developer organization or sandbox so that you can debug code[4].

- QA orgs - One or more organizations for those doing quality assurance and testing. Outside QA will typically be done

---

[4] The IDE and ANT also make it easy to push code quickly into another organization, but an unmanaged package also makes it easy to remove the code when you are finished.

using an installed package. But inside QA, where you don't' mind testers seeing the code, will at least part of the time be done on an org that contains the source. That makes it possible for your developers to log into the QA org to see problems and try fixes on the org itself – something that is not possible with a managed package. You'll need a set of orgs for each type of organization you are targeting – group, professional, enterprise, etc.

- Deployment org – The main org from which the managed package is deployed. Never test on this org (other than running unit tests), and don't create any objects or fields on this org that are not part of the package. All code on this org should have passed QA and be checked in if using source control.

- Patch orgs – Supported for managed applications on the AppExchange, these are used for point releases.

- Security Review org – A separate developer org on which you have installed your managed package for the AppExchange security review.

- Two person account orgs – If you are supporting person accounts you will need one person account org that contains the source code for testing and debugging, and another on which to install the managed package for testing and QA.

- Other feature specific orgs – You will need at least one and sometimes two orgs to test specific features, such as multiple currency support. In some cases you can combine features to reduce the number of organizations.

- Limit test org – This will probably be a full enterprise sandbox if you are an ISV partner, though in some cases you can get by with a developer org. This is a QA org on which you load large amounts of data to test your application's readiness to deploy to larger organizations. Try to have at least a few hundred thousand records of each type that your application works with – over a million is better.

- Bug sharing org – See the section on Using Salesforce.com support later in this chapter.

With Sharing

Use the With Sharing option on all VisualForce controllers. If you need to bypass sharing rules, call into another class that does not have with sharing defined.

This applies primarily to VisualForce controllers.

This will help you pass security review.

Watch for Older Software When Deploying

Some of the organizations that you deploy to may have applications that have not been updated in a while. This can potentially lead to unexpected interactions with your software.

One classic example relates to custom settings. It is not uncommon to use custom settings to save application information. However, on API version 17 and earlier, any attempt to perform a regular DML after modifying a custom setting can lead to a MIXED_DML_OPERATION error. That means that if you have a trigger that modifies a custom setting, and it is followed by a trigger in another application running on API version 17 or earlier that performs a DML operation, you can see this error.

Given that API version 17 dates back to 2009, it's not unreasonable to require customers to update older software. It's just something to be aware of.

Salesforce.com Updates

Salesforce updates their software three times a year. Actually, that's not quite accurate – the platform is updated with minor bug fixes much more often, but those changes are unpredictable and rarely cause a problem.

In theory, the behavior of your application will remain unchanged as long as you keep the API version the same. In practice, that doesn't always work. With so many possible sets of software features, organization metadata, system configurations, and third party applications running different API versions, it's almost miraculous that anything works at all.

Be sure to have at least one sandbox ready to be updated to the next release preview as soon as it is available. Sign up for pre-release preview orgs on those releases where they are available. Deploy your code on the preview sandbox as soon as possible and verify that all unit tests pass. Perform a manual test of all Visual-Force pages. If your tests pass and the pages function correctly, you can breathe a sigh of relief – chances are good your application will work on the next release. Until then, continue to do QA in preparation for the release.

Do not change the API version of your software during this preview period other than perhaps to do initial experiments on a separate preview organization. Do not change the API version of the software on your deployment org until after everyone has been upgraded to the next release. Otherwise you risk running into a situation where you cannot deploy urgent updates.

Change API versions of your software between Salesforce.com releases if you wish. Don't feel you have to stay in sync with Salesforce. Update the API version of your application when Force.com incorporates new features that you want to use. Be sure to perform a full QA cycle when you update the API version of your application – that is where you are more likely to see behavior changes in your application (as compared to platform updates where your software stays on the same API version).

Using Salesforce.com Support

The Force.com platform is large and complex, which means that it, like any large and complex software platform, has bugs. The day may come where you will find one.

Your first step should be to search Google, the appropriate section of the Force.com forums, and salesforce.stackexchange.com to see if anyone else has run into the same problem and has a workaround. Most of the time, this will be the case.

Check the Salesforce known issues site (currently at http://success.salesforce.com/issues_index but you can always just search for "Salesforce known issues") to see if it is a known platform bug.

If you don't find any helpful information (which is more likely if you are using a newer or less frequently used feature on the platform), try the following:

- Find a way to reproduce the issue, preferably on a clean or relatively clean developer org that is dedicated to demonstrating bugs.
- Document in the simplest possible terms a set of step by step instructions to reproduce the bug. Use screenshots where possible.
- Submit a case. Include the org ID and specify that you have granted Salesforce login access to the developer org where you have reproduced the problem.
- Once again, provide the org ID and specify that you have granted login access, in response to the request for this in-

formation that will inevitably come from the person assigned to your case. Don't think about why you are being
asked for this again when you included it in the original request, it will just cause you more stress.

- Depending on who you are, you may get a response indicating that they really aren't interested in hearing about
platform bugs unless you purchase premium support.
Whether this is because only people who purchase premium support are capable of finding platform bugs, or due to
some other reason, is unknown.

- If you are lucky, you will quickly receive an explanation of
an error that you made in your code, and you will somewhat sheepishly thank the support agent and the case will
be closed.

- Otherwise, you will wait for a period of time (hours? days)
and possibly several exchanges while the agent reproduces
and comes to understand the problem and is convinced
that yes, it is a real problem that should be referred to tier
3 support.

- You will receive a message that your case has been forwarded to tier 3 support and that you will be notified as
soon as there is additional information.

- You will receive a message that your case has been forwarded to tier 3 support and that you will be notified as
soon as there is additional information.

- You will receive a message that your case has been forwarded to tier 3 support and that you will be notified as
soon as there is additional information.

- You will be notified either that the bug you found is either
"by design" and is thus a feature, or that it is a bug that
they are aware of, so the case will be closed and you will be
notified if it is ever fixed.

- You will never be notified, even if the bug if fixed.

Ok, I'm being just a little bit mean here. The support agents are actually a very nice group of people. The problem is, they spend a lot of their time answering beginner's issues, and it takes a while for them to sort out tougher problems. That filtering is part of their job, for all that it can be frustrating.

Sometimes, especially if you've identified a bug during the release preview period, you'll get a lot of quick action on a case — as that's the period when they really are trying to track down and solve any breaking changes on the platform.

Keep in mind that this sequence is subject to change at any time, as Salesforce.com support policies do change. If you're curious what kind of support you qualify for, you can always submit a case and find out...

Here's a hint. If you think you've found a real platform bug, at the same time as you submit the case, post a question to the relevant Force.com forum and on salesforce.stackexchange.com. Note that you think it may be a platform bug.

If you are lucky, your post will be noticed by someone from Salesforce.com — a number of them monitor the forums. If so, you will have the pleasure of communicating directly with someone who will understand what you are saying, be able to look at and understand your steps to reproduce the problem, and work directly with the people responsible for solving the problem (in fact, he or she may be the person responsible for solving the problem). In that case, not only may you get a forecast for when the problem will be fixed, you may even be notified when it has been fixed and asked to verify if the fix works.

Finally, don't wait for them to solve your problem. It's almost always possible to come up with a workaround.

Conclusion

At the start of this book I made a promise – that it would not be a rehash of the Force.com documentation. I think I've kept that promise. It is my hope that developers at all levels will find this book a good companion to the other developer resources that are available. I know that it is not a replacement for those resources, and that is by intent.

This book contains all of the things that I wish I had known a few years ago when I began the transition from part-time Apex consultant to full time Apex application developer. But, like you, I'm still learning. And the platform continues to change. Fortunately, thanks to modern publishing technology, this book can change as well. Many of the things I learned over the past year have been incorporated into this second edition. I have no doubt there will be a third someday.

So here is my invitation to you – I would love to hear your view of what topics or contents should go in future editions of the book. I'd also be glad to hear of additional best-practices and design patterns, or even places where you disagree with my conclusions. After all, the term "best practices" only means that set of practices that are, in the opinion of experienced developers, the best ways to solve certain problems.

Contact me via Email at dan@desawarepublishing.com

Or follow me on twitter at @danappleman

Remember you can view any corrections to the book at www.advancedapex.com and download the sample code at www.advancedapex.com/samplecode

Acknowledgements and Dedication

The genesis of this book started several years ago in a conversation with George Hu, currently the COO at Salesforce.com, in which one of the topics we discussed was why many developers had a difficult time with limits and what could be done to help them. I wasn't ready to do anything about it at the time, but I never forgot the conversation, and I knew, even then, that when I did have the time and sufficient expertise, that would be the first subject I would want to tackle. Thanks, George.

Others at Salesforce.com who helped include Adam Seligman, Steve Bobrowski and Mario Korf, whose enthusiastic support and comments encouraged me to push forward on the way towards publication. Thanks to Michael Floyd for strong-arming me into accelerating work on this second edition. Thanks also to Domenique Sillett Buxton for her inspiration.

I'm deeply grateful to Don Robins, Adam Purkiss, David Watson, David Claiborne and Jon Kilburn who offered great technical and general feedback. I look forward to continuing our conversations.

This book is dedicated to the team at Full Circle CRM. They continue to tolerate me taking time to work on this book while I could have been developing more product features. That said, I do think there is some value in that when people look at our product, our sales people will be able to hold up this book and say: "this is how we built it", and hopefully convey a sense of the effort and technology we put into developing a world-class application. And, if you have moment, point your marketing team to www.fullcirclecrm.com. I think they'll like what they see.

About the cover

Funny story. The previous edition cover featured a sign "Caution, Software Ahead" that was a riff on the Salesforce "No Software" logo. What I didn't realize at the time is that when Salesforce said "No Software" they didn't mean no software development (in the sense of you can do your development entirely in the user interface), but no software in the sense of not having to install and maintain software on your machine. Which goes to show that the way marketing messages are interpreted really does depend on the audience. With the Force.com platform's evolution into a software development platform, that logo, and the first edition cover, are both good candidates for retirement.

For this edition we chose a Penrose triangle, representing something that is very real, but not quite what seems at first glance. And if that doesn't describe the Apex language, I don't know what does.

Online Courses by Dan Appleman

Dan Appleman has also published a variety of courses online at Pluralsight.com. These include:

Career and Survival Strategies for Software Developers

Introduction to Leadership and Management for Developers

So You Want to be an Entrepreneur?

Force.com and Apex Fundamentals for Developers

Force.com for .NET Developers

Pluralsight also offers additional Apex and Force.com courses by well-known experts like Don Robins, Adam Purkiss, Richard Seroter and Matt Lacey.

Visit Pluralsight.com for more information and to obtain a free trial subscription.

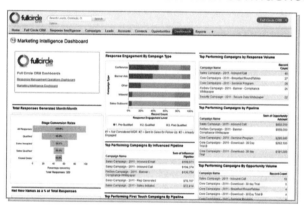

Also from Desaware Publishing:

In addition to developing software, Dan Appleman has spent over 20 years volunteering with a youth leadership program. If you have teens, work with them, or even manage a software development team, you'll learn valuable leadership skills and how to teach them with this unique book.

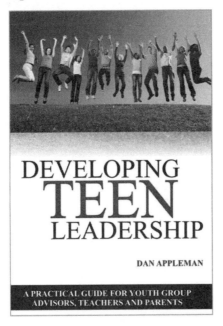

Not long ago, all it took to have a comfortable career was to do well in high school, get a college degree, and find a nice stable job. But today, good grades are not enough.

But there remain endless opportunities for those with real leadership skills - regardless of career choice.

Developing Teen Leadership covers virtually every topic today's parents, teachers and youth advisors need to help teens gain the leadership skills they will need in today's rapidly changing world.

www.teenleadershipbook.com

Notes

Notes

Notes

Notes

Notes

Notes